Redneck Spirituality

—Books One & Two—
Combined Edition

Redneck Spirituality

Combined Edition
—Book One—
Don't Paint Your Turds Pink

&

—Book Two—
If Shit's In Your Face—Something's Stinkin' In Your Thinkin'

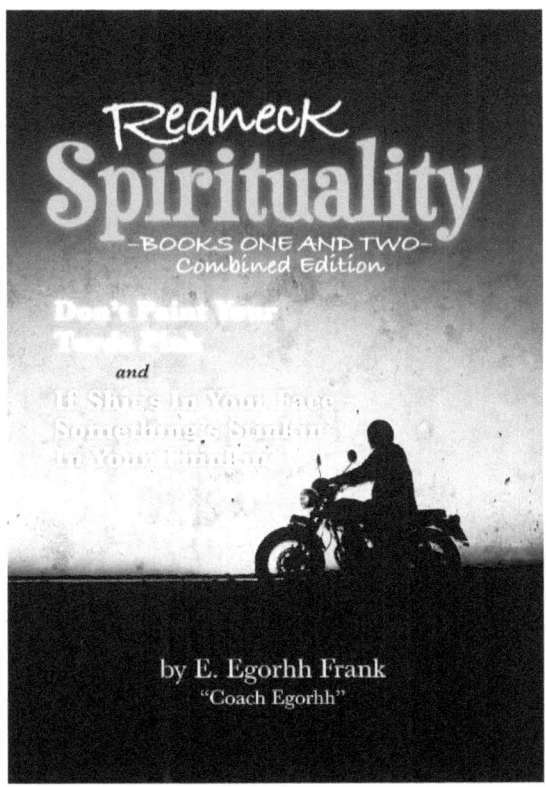

by
E. Egorhh Frank
"Coach Egorhh"

Copyright 2018
by Edmond E. Frank
All rights reserved.
No part of this book may be reproduced
by any means or in any form without
the express permission of the author.
KDP Paperback
ISBN—978-1-7327328-6-5

Table of Contents

BOOK ONE

Dedication
Epitaph
Acknowledgments
About the Author
Introduction

Part 1—*Life's Laws*

3	Life's Laws (listed)
7	Let's Talk About the Truth—
9	So What's This Writer's Agenda?
13	Take Your Time
15	Some Things You Need to Know
17	How Am I Doing?

Part 2—*Reflections of Life*

21	Peeling Onions
23	Omissions
25	Pity
26	One Single Lie
27	Actors In a Play
28	What Is
29	Destiny
30	Needs—Part One
31	Needs—Part Two
33	Needs—Part Three
35	A Cry in the Dark
36	Bug Brains

37	Playing It Safe
38	Reflections of Ourselves
40	A Good Day . . .
41	Thoughts Create
42	We Always Know
43	Integrity
44	All that I Am
45	About Changing
46	Think for Yourself
47	Faulting You
48	About Limitations
49	Fools
50	The Gift of Our Pain
51	In the Face of One's Pain
52	Selfish
54	What Is Right and Wrong
55	The Smallness of Our Mind
56	The Gift in Evil
57	Lessons
58	Death of a Different Sort
59	Into Her Care
61	Man's Greatest Danger
62	My Greatest Aspiration
63	The Sting of Truth
64	Always!
65	On the Line
66	About Apologies
68	Anger
69	The Root Element of Wisdom
70	Being "Normal"
71	Perfect Perception
72	Count on Yourself
73	Weird
74	Change Your Mind—Change Your Life
75	Fearlessness of Innocence
76	Fear
77	Standing by Your Beliefs

78	Whole and Healed
79	Standards
80	Illusions of Security
81	Accept
83	Adults Do
84	Generations Past
85	Who You Really Are
86	Our Own Reality
87	Our World
88	About Blame
89	Being Who You Are
90	Right or Wrong
91	The Words We Use
92	Thoughts
94	Commitment
95	Death's Whisper
96	A Weapon of Fear
97	There in Balance
98	Its Lies
99	About Liars
100	Endless Possibilities
101	The Works of Others
102	No One's World is the Same
103	Taking Offense
104	Selfish Wants
105	Conventional Thinking
106	Wants and Demands
107	Maturity
108	Ticklish
109	The Blind Spot
110	Participation
112	To Be Cherished
113	Being Authentic
114	The Last Haunt
115	Epilogue
116	The Assessment
117	One Last Thing

BOOK TWO

119	Book Two Title Page
120	Note
121	Dedication
122	Epitaph
123	Acknowledgments
124	Introduction

Part 1—*Life's Laws*

129	About the Laws
131	The Spiritual Laws of Life (26 listed)
136	The Bottom Line
139	To Set You Up To Win

Part 2—*About Life*

143	The Wonderment
144	My Shit Don't Stink
146	About Pink Paint
148	Admissions Price
149	The Need to be Accepted
150	Acceptance
151	Adoption
152	On the Law of Present Living
154	Feces
155	Squeezing Oranges
156	Roots
158	Social Creatures
159	No Secrets
160	The Two-Sided Mirror
162	A Gifted Few
163	About Respect and Disrespect
164	The Currency of Esteem
165	Vet to Vet

166	Support
167	Waiting on a Friend
168	Validations
169	The Sting of Truth
170	Pretense
171	Expensive People
172	No Fear
173	You Are the Teacher
174	Forgiveness—The Stupid Shit
176	Then There Is FORGIVENESS—The Serious Shit
179	Little Flying Lizards
180	Tigers
181	Feeding Frenzy
182	One's Way of Life
183	About Song
184	Courage
185	Earning Respect
186	Needs and Wants
188	My Viewpoint—In Redneck Speak
191	About Offensive People

Part 3—*Reflections of Love*

195	Unconditional Love
196	Accepting
198	About Relationships
199	Odd Thoughts
200	The Truth About Commitment
202	About Proving One's Love
203	Magnets
205	The Truth About Love
206	The Journey of the Heart
208	Living to Our Joy
210	I'm Okay
211	The Other Half of Loving Is Accepting
212	Love and Acceptance
213	Driving a Relationship

214	Control Is Never Love
215	Giving
216	No freedom—No Love
217	The Way You Want It
219	Ultimatums
220	The Relationship Game
221	Giving and Accepting
222	Diamonds
223	Relationships—Needs & Soul Mates
224	Soul Mates
227	Lovegasm
228	Working At A Relationship
229	A Single Man's Prayer
230	Fearful Needs
231	In the End
233	Perfect Love
234	The Flashbulb of Love
235	Sex Is A Beautiful Thing
238	In the Energy
240	Saying It With Love
241	F.U.C.K.
242	Grit Your Teeth and Buck Up

Part 4—*About Politics*

247	The Collective Consciousness
249	Which Side of the Fence
250	Left Turn—Right Turn
252	Liberals, Conservatives & Spiritual Laws
254	Repeating History

Part 5—*Organized Religion, Spirituality, and a Higher Power*

259	The Ocean of God
260	The Truth of Our Being
261	Putting the Shame on Sex

262	Good and Evil?
264	It's All Good
266	Free Thinkers
268	Shepherds and Sheep
269	The Ego's Expectations
270	Resurrections
271	Designated Creator
272	Everything We Need
273	Soul Experience
274	In Our Hearts
276	Enlightenment and the Spiritual Warrior
277	Shining Moments
278	Religion
279	Chicken Exits
281	Your Conscious Choice
282	About Beliefs
283	You Are the Winner
286	Now On to the Next Lottery
288	The Choice
290	The Taste-Buds of God
295	One and the Same
297	Epilogue
301	About the Assessment
303	The Assessment
307	About the Author

Redneck Spirituality
—Book One—

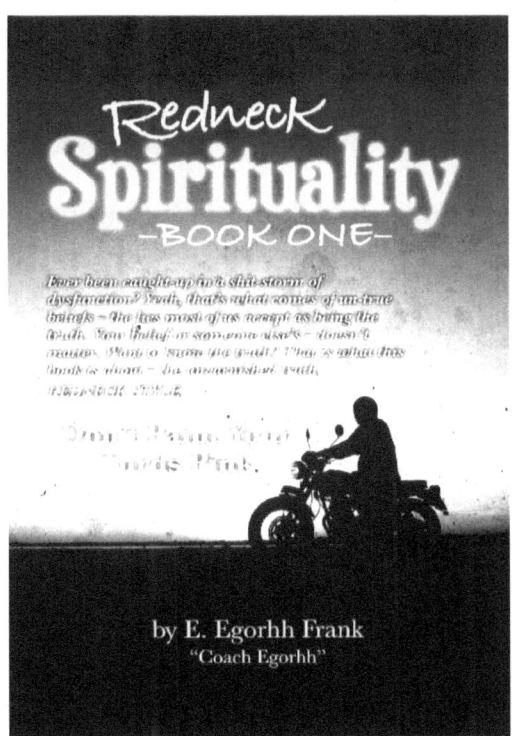

Don't Paint Your Turds Pink

Dedication

For the one who has given my life—life!
He has taught me to live true to myself
in authenticity and honesty:
The two things that it takes for a man to know,
and to respect himself.

My journey has been one of magnificence and wonder
with him, an ever-present presence—
my silent, invisible companion, dear friend, and mentor.

Glimpsing life through his perspective has been a privilege.
I dedicate this book to

The Angel

Epitaph

There are no coincidences.
Your life is run by your soul and everything
put before you is for your learning.

It is no mistake that something about this book
has attracted your attention.

Your soul knows there is something
for you here that you need.

— Coach Egorhh

Acknowledgments

The Las Vegas Creative Writing Critique Group:
Most were not in this venue, and some were resistant to the content. When you offer a perspective that is this different from the way most have been taught to see life, well, you just don't know where folks will take it. The critiques I received there were some of the most valuable.

The main reason most authors write is to touch the reader. The reader may choose to like what is written, or they may hate it. Either way, the writer has touched them and given them cause to think.

As an author, it is only those who don't give a shit who I've failed. So THANKS to you folks out in Summerlin for giving a shit—for allowing me to touch you, figuratively, of course.

The Sin City Critique Group:
Only a few were not of this venue (searching to understand and to make their lives better). Of those who were not, they were more loving and accepting—and open-minded.

They showed me where normal folks go when they aren't being led to stampede. And they helped me to write in ways to be better understood—and they did it with a sense of humor.

Their critiques were also very valuable, and mostly enjoyable. The times they weren't enjoyable were when I most needed to pay attention.

Thanks to my Beta Readers—too numerous to list here. I hope I added as much to your lives as you did mine.

To Bobby Daniels Graphics who did all the excellent work setting up the cover—a real artist.

And lastly, to my editors:

> **Toni Briegel**
> **Kitty Schuler**
> **Denise Sage**

Thank you all for the excellence of your advice.

Introduction

Again, this book is about Spiritual Laws, the indelible truths of life—
WHOA!
Hey, just hold that thought. If you are like me, and someone comes along and tries to saddle me with some "law" or "truth" I might not agree with—well, that's about the time my pucker string gets *reee-aal* tight.

I get that—So feel free to call them *principals*, or *truisms*, whatever turns your crank. Thing is, like the physical *Law of Gravity*, they too *just are*. Ignore gravity, and you are going to take a fall. Ignore these truths—these Spiritual Laws of Life—and no matter what you call them, your life will take the fall. The cuts and scrapes, the broken bones on which you hobble through life—those are called dysfunctions. Take a deep breath, loosen up that pucker string, and go with it.

Now, just knowing something in your head is like looking at it *out there*, and changes nothing. Knowing it in your heart is like looking at it *in here*—from the heart's perspective—a completely different life-changing way of seeing it.

* * *

It's one thing to sit on the cliff over a deep sandstone canyon, and to look down at the Moki Indian dwellings tucked up under the overhanging wall. Seeing the tops of the cottonwood trees way down there in the bottom of that dry wash, you know that down there somewhere, there is water—and you're damned thirsty!

It's quite another thing to edge your way along the narrow ledges, the hot sun on your back making your shirt stick, and sweat trickle down into your butt-crack as you inch your way along with your ass hanging out over the abyss. It's a fear-filled journey to get to those dwellings under the overhanging cliff and to stand in the doorways of what's left of those rock and mud homes.

You look down at the ancient fingerprints still etched into that centuries-old dried mud. Then, down at the sand and pebbles mixed with flint chips from the making of arrowheads, you realize you are standing on sacred ground. You climb on down to the wash below using the foot and hand hollows cut centuries ago with stone tools, now allowing you to negotiate your way down that last near-vertical wall.

Ah, but there is freedom in treading the ancient paths in the cool shade of those majestic cliffs with their black skirts of manganese stains—and then to drink cool, sweet spring water from the same natural sandstone cistern where the long-dead Moki once drank.

* * *

That is what it is like to take that famous "eighteen-inch journey" between your head and your heart—to know something in your heart. It's not a mental thing—it's a scary, experiential/emotional/spiritual thing.

Section Two is about experiencing these Laws of Truth from the heart. Truths that also are ancient, long-kept secrets hidden away by the leaders and preachers of our society—truths they replaced with lies to keep you enslaved to their own agendas. *It is **NO** lie that the truth will set you free.*

In this book are listed the sixteen truths I think are the most important. There are many more, but these are a good beginning. These laws, if taken to heart and followed, will give you a new life and freedom such that you likely cannot now conceive. If by living these truths, a redneck like me can mend the broken bones of his own life's dysfunctions, so too can you. Or perhaps you would rather wait to meet the Angel—we all do eventually. Y'know?

Surely you know that the Angel doesn't give many reprieves. But at a time when I was desperate to know the truth about life, he gave me the answers—and I discovered the courage to make that journey. I now pass on his truth to you. The courage this takes can only be found within yourselves. So from The Angel, to me, and now to you:

Here is your reprieve....

I offer it to you—*without expectations.* And that, folks, that "without expectations" part, is the definition of a true gift. Accept this redneck's book—this gift—or don't. It's up to you.

You are the Creator of your life!

Book One
PART ONE

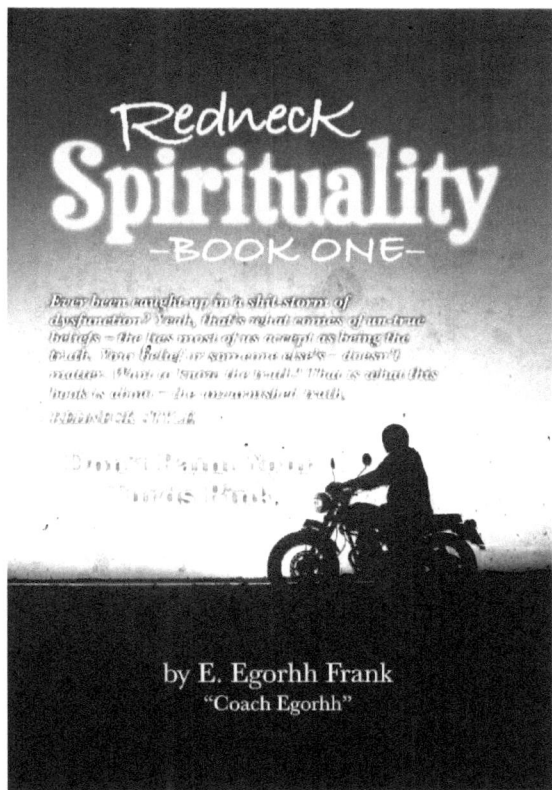

Life's Laws
The Truths of Life

➢ ..

NOTE:
You will likely want to refer back to this section occasionally. Consider placing a page marker on this page for easy referencing. Markers can be purchased at any stationary store, or you can fold a piece of tape at the edge to make your own.

The Laws of Life

1—I am the Creator.
Most only take this to mean I create my own life. That is true. But to own it requires me to understand that there is nothing in my life that I have not had the deciding factor in creating. It is true, too, that all other Spiritual Laws presented here are just aspects of this one. As you read through and comprehend the concepts in this book, you will get a sense of how this Law touches upon the infinite. This is your life, and these are its truths.

2—Thoughts create.
Look around you. Everything our species ever created began as a thought in someone's mind. As for the rest, there is an order to the universe. One that speaks to sentience—to feeling, sensing, understanding, creating—like us, but much more. It is a "Higher Power" infinitely beyond what our religions can conceive.

3—Thoughts are energy.
In being our own Creator, we choose in every second of life, the energy with which we are creating. It can only be one of two energies—the energy of **all that is love**, or the energy of **all** that is not love (fear).

4—The energy out returns in kind.
The energy of your every thought determines what comes to you in life—*love* or *fear*. This is that freedom of choice which is our greatest gift of all Creation. It is this choice that creates the path of our lives and the quality with which we walk.

5—The Universe always balances.
With every sorrowful thing, there is the potential for an equal joy, yet we are the creators in our lives. There is equal joy to be found in every sorrowful event *If* we will look for *and* accept it. The truth is, it is we

who have chosen the sorrow, and it is we who must seek and choose the joy. The potential for both exists in balance within the universe, and we are but a shift of mind away, requiring no more struggle than the acceptance of our next breath.

6—*The energy of thoughts must flow.*
Once taken in, the energy of fear stays and is the initial cause of all sickness *if* it is not felt, acknowledged, and then released. Even love energy must be released—given back out—in order to flow.

7—*Along with being the creator comes responsibility—one cannot BE the Creator and play the blame game.*
One cannot *not* create. Each person must accept responsibility for the totality of creating their life, especially for all thoughts and feelings associated in that process. ***Blame is the abdication of responsibility, perhaps the greatest of all Mankind's dysfunctional lies.***

8—*The world is not "out there"—it is "in here."*
It is comprised of every thought, every belief, and every feeling you have. Your world is totally your responsibility because you are the only one who has the ability to respond—the ability to make it better or worse, loving or fearful. ***Only you can change your mind.***

9—*Others are but a mirror for us to see ourselves.*
What we don't like in others is but the reflection of what we don't like in ourselves. If it were not also within us, we could never see it in them.

10—*The purpose of life is for those lessons.*
When we refuse the learning, the lessons will be presented again, more forcefully, until we learn them—or die.

11—Self-esteem requires integrity—it is the respect of your soul.
What our heart feels, what we think, say, and do—all must align as the same, and be coupled with the strength of intention to be in integrity. Integrity commands esteem.

12—Our lives are run primarily by our needs, then by our wants.
As such, our lives are mostly run from an unconscious level. We all know what it is we want—few know what we need to have it. Needs are about the necessities—wants are about the quality.

13—Our life is our sole possession—and so it is for everyone.
We, being the Creator, have all the say in creating our own life—no say in the creation of anyone else's. They are always free to be, say, or do whatever they want—without actual harm to others.

14—Change is the constant of the universe.
Change is fearful. With everything we find fearful, change—the unknown—will be at its core. Fear? Fear is *not* a constant. It is a choice (Law 3). And sometimes, it is a barometer for change.

15—To create a functional life requires one to do one's own thinking.
The beliefs passed down through the generations, as well as by our religions, are generally accepted as truth. Even when those "truths" serve us falsely, few have the courage to think for themselves. It takes great courage to think differently in the face of family and/or religion. Dysfunction will always come when living the lies passed down to you by others.

16—Controlling anything outside ourselves is a fallacy.
We can only control another inasmuch as they will let us—or rather, pretend to let us. And our world? See Law 8. Yes, we control our own world, because it lies within us.

Let's Talk About the Truth—

So these laws are the truths governing life—the ones some would call Spiritual Laws? But for many, "spiritual" is another way of saying "religious." This book is not about religion. That is not to say it does not recognize a "Higher Power."

Truth always uplifts. But lies—lies drive your life into the ground. The problem is, we have all been taught a boatload of lies—well-meaning mostly—but lies. All have come from the people we trust the most. It is the same story for nearly everyone. Will you be one of the few to question, who will have the audacity to seek out the truth? Most won't. Most will accept those crash landings, and the resulting broken bones, and keep on hobbling through life on their dysfunctions—no courage in that, just painful ignorance.

For some, the mere sight of the ground rushing up to meet them makes them reach out for the truth. For others, it is the crash, the burning chaos, and the ensuing ashes that send them searching like a Phoenix for a way to rebuild their lives better. For others like me, it is nothing less than the *Grim Reaper*, the *Angel of Death,* who forces us to look at our lies. By then, it is usually too late. We generally go to our graves with a whimper or a wail, despising ourselves for never having had the courage to search out the truth about life—especially, our own—and to *accept* that truth.

Looking back, one can see so much clearly. When looking from a depth of six feet, that statement is no longer such a cliché. Yet even then, very few reach out and grasp their courage, cover themselves with its mantle, and refuse the Angel. That is what it takes to *win* a reprieve—*and evolve.* Not many reach, not many cover, not many win.

And evolve? I have proposed it as in "accepting," and even "winning." Evolving in this life for you may be about "grasping"—**taking this reprieve**. If you wait for the Angel, likely it will be too late.

Melodramatic?—Maybe.

Still, no matter where you are in the order of all this, that you have this book in your hands says your soul believes there is something here you need. It is your soul that, in every moment of life, is providing you with the lessons. These truths may not appear to be all that earth-shattering.

Neither is the cocoon of a chrysalis—a soon-to-be butterfly. Make no mistake: These laws are a life-changing cocoon for you, the chrysalis, to evolve—and for the rest of your life, be a butterfly.

So What's This Author's Agenda?

Again, these Laws "just are." They don't need your approval—nor do I. My agenda here is merely to expose you to these truths.

Some will recognize their validity and accept them. They will change their minds *right now*, and their lives, also, *right now*. Others won't. Still, exposing you to the truth will make you aware of the lies you never knew you believed—until *right now*. It may well take more pain and dysfunction in your life to convince you. That is your choice—again—*right now!*

"Right now"—do you wonder why I keep hammering on these two words? It is because, as one who knows, *right now* is the only time there is—the only time you are guaranteed. Like I once did, **most folks waste it.**

Have you noticed how these laws are interwoven—like a cocoon? Just so, the concepts—beginning in Part Two—often involve aspects of more than one law. No need to memorize, it is only in knowing what they *mean* that you will know anything. The aim of the concepts is to show you that meaning—what life looks like in the reflection of the laws. If you don't understand something, the applicable laws are listed in an abbreviated form. Go back to the long explanations and re-read the laws as needed.

As a teenager, I once lived in a construction camp for a dam on the Acheloos River in Greece. My brother, Mark, and I often swam in that river, down in a gorge where the surface seemed to be almost still—although we knew there was a considerable volume of flow. Looking into the dark depths of the river there, that was clearly a given. My greatest wish for you is that the flow of this book will feel as deep to you now as the Acheloos River felt to me then.

Some will plunge right into the cooling waters of this book. Some will not. Sharing these truths with someone searching is helping. Saving is NOT my purpose. No one drowns in these waters. So, dabble your feet in the coolness of this river, or dive right in. Maybe you'd rather just stand on the bank and sweat. It's up to you

Every good book needs a hero. This time, that hero must be you. The simple truth is:

> **When you change your mind about anything,
> you change your whole life—forever!**

Frightening . . . isn't it? Do you see why I say **"hero?"** Yes, it does require courage. This is why so few people make the changes they say they want in their lives.

Again, to hammer it home one last time—my purpose here is to expose you to the truth. That you accept it and evolve—or not—is up to you. That part does not belong under any hammer in my hand. Many simply lack the courage. No matter how painful their life, they know it well. More comfortable is the pain of their known dysfunction than the fear of an unknown change.

> **Are you one of the few with the courage to change
> and—like a butterfly—discover the beauty within yourself?**

My hammer is now in your own hand—the gift within this book. Every nail—every true belief—you choose to hammer home will bring new joy into your life. Choose now to have the courage to change.

> **Can you not see that every caterpillar makes this same choice?
> And butterflies—do you think they ever have regrets?**

It is hard to be a fresh voice writing about Spiritual Laws and concepts that have been around all through the ages. Even the ancient Greek philosopher, Socrates, talked about them.

> *"The unexamined life is not worth living."*—**Socrates**

Examining and understanding who you are and what your true responsibilities in life are is the crux of these Laws of Life.

Fresh? Different? What does this book have to offer that all those before it didn't? Perhaps it is the fact that in the past there have been few writers with the cajones to say it like it is—much easier, and profitable, to give you a feelie-good book to read. This is a workbook.

> **This is NOT a feelie-good workbook!**

Can you ever have change by only looking at what feels good and supports you in your thinking? Your thinking creates your life—all, of it. If there is dysfunction in your life, it can only mean there is dysfunction in your thinking. Telling you things that feel good only validates your thinking—the functional and the dysfunctional, and changes nothing.

The things that can and do change your life are those that ***don't*** feel good. These Spiritual Laws are the truth. If you are living a lie, seeing the truth will always be uncomfortable because it demands change. Change never feels good until after it becomes the known normal. Decide now if you want it. Again, living a dysfunctional life may not be all that enjoyable, but it does feel safer than making changes. Now, let's talk about the lies.

It is not "politically correct" to tell you just how badly your life has been "anal-lyzed." Shit! If you've even begun to accept these Laws of Truth, then you cannot help but begin seeing those dysfunctional lies—the ones you have been taught upon which you "should" base your life.

> ***It might help to know that "should" is merely the shit from between someone's ears—usually not your own—and it stinks.***

If it stinks, why would we accept it? Face it—no one finds the smell of their own shit all that repulsive. Well, do you? If you did, it would make it difficult to live with yourself, now wouldn't it? It's only other people's shit that we think stinks—no matter out of which end it comes. Perhaps that is why we never look at ourselves when making changes. We only look "out there" and try to change them.

When it's coming from one's own end, you might pinch your nose and accept it, but when coming from the other—the end of "authority"—we seldom do our own thinking, but rather pinch the nose of our mind. Their mental shit then becomes your own, and you don't notice the stink.

Politics be damned! It also begs repeating—clearly—who those liars are that wiped all that "should" off onto your life. They are **your *parents*, your *religions*, *the leaders of society*—*nearly all those whom you love or respect*.**

Why else would you accept those lies without question? Just know, it was never a deliberate thing. They, too, pinched the nose of their mind—accepted it all before you—same as you. What if the person telling you all that "should" had been someone you didn't even know—some redneck, maybe like me?

Yes, puts it all in a different light—doesn't it? However, with me, you are free to think for yourself and to question every word you read. Hell, I encourage you to question everything between these pages.

And the "should" between your own ears—is it your own? Does it uplift and nourish you with truth? The thing about shit is that it results from what has nourished you. What makes it stink so badly is when it comes from between someone else's ears and has never nourished. Instead, it has made you a stinking victim in life.

Now to be honest, didn't I just tell you how ***your life has been*** "anal-lyzed"—how you have been a "stinking victim?"

> **Whoa, hey! Have I also been "should-ing" on you—**
> **Or am I offering you a choice?**

The key words here are **"...your life has been"**—**PAST TENSE!** Point is, that was the truth about your past. It is now up to you if that will be the truth in your future. Within the cocoon of these Spiritual Laws, that victimized pupa from your past now has a chance to become a butterfly.

Me? What do I get for rubbing all this truth in your face? I fully expect *some* will want to crucify me. Hell, Socrates was put to death for this same act of politically incorrect social disobedience. My purpose in sharing these truths with you is simply to offer you an opportunity to make your world—and mine—a little better place.

I have no desire to be a preacher or guru. I'm just tired of seeing this shit-storm of dysfunction swirling all around, and knowing the reasons behind it all—and yet not caring enough to open my mouth and risk condemnation. Twenty-five years ago, the Angel gave me a reprieve. This book and the one (or more) to follow, just may be his reason.

Take your time

This is not a big book, but if you're paying attention, it will be a long read. It is meant to be a workbook.

Some will read this book for the information, and some will do the work. It all depends on whether they came to this game to be spectators in the bleachers or players on the field of life.

It doesn't matter whether it is hard copy or digital. To work with it, you will need a notebook, preferably one that is a ring binder—at some point, you may need to add a page or three.

Currently, this is Book One of Two—one binder will do. In the beginning, write only on the right-hand pages. The reason for this will be explained later. Write down the title and page number of the reflection, then answer the questions, do the exercises, and write down your own thoughts.

If you have no personal opinion—it's okay, you will soon. This is about self-discovery, and what you discover will be huge. Some will buy this book and read it for the information. They want knowledge—they don't want change.

The *bad* news first: *You will get change.*

The *good* news? Yes, you guessed it: *You will get change*. And, it will be the change you want.

And the *truth: There is no good or bad*—we'll discuss that later. For now, here is one clue. "Good and bad" reside only between your ears.

I guarantee that if you WORK this workbook, your life will be different—better. Maybe, you will make a difference for someone else, perhaps even one of those whom you love.

Without you, they may never have a clue about those lies. Pass this book on, or better yet, get another and pass that one on. The debt everyone owes to that Higher Power for the privilege of being alive *is to live a life that makes a difference.*

Could be that—like me—*now's your chance.*

Some Things You Need to Know

To this author, being a redneck means he has always lived life on the cusp of crudity. This book *says it like it is* with *in-your-face crudity*. This is the redneck way. Much of this material cries for just that approach. For the most part, the language used will be as clearly written as this redneck can write it.

You have read the Laws—benign, don't you think? Now it's time to look at what they mean in life. This is where things may start not-feeling-so-benign. *This* is where you will start seeing that your viewpoint of life may not be the truth. *This* is where you will start seeing the lies you have been taught to believe.

Some of the following reflections will merely feel "off,"—is the writer redneck challenged? Maybe. *Some* will tweak your sense of propriety. *Some* you may feel are outrageously blasphemous.

Good!

As all speak to your own perceptions, these are the things that you need to look at—the ones that mean change for your life—if you accept them. Fact is, your soul sees the truth in them, but your conscious mind sees only the change they require in your life, *and is afraid.* You now have only one of two ways to go:

> *Gather your courage and change. Or accept whatever dysfunctions you have going—and stop right here.*

The fact remains, you have already been exposed to the laws—to the truth. If the lies you've been taught are not yet apparent, they soon will be—right in your face. Your soul will see to it. Again, it is your soul that brought you to these pages. If any peace, love, or joy is missing for you—and you want it—then gather your courage *and keep on reading.*

Bottom line:
I may be the only person who has the right—even the obligation—to say this last thing to you. This is because,

I have been there.

When the Angel comes to take you home, he will either pick up a hero or a coward. That is the choice you have before you—
RIGHT NOW.

>>><<<

How am I Doing?

This is a workbook. When finished, likely you'll feel a need to know how you did. If you aren't interested in scoring yourself, then you've failed—failed to be honest.

Face it: This book would not be in your hands—or digitally in your face—if you did not want something from it. Here is what I am asking you to do. Make the following notations near the title of each reflection, either in your hardcover or notebook.

1. With every reflection presented, if you agree without resistance, just put a checkmark.
These are things that were in your belief system, to begin with.
(✓)

2. If the reflection has pointed out something more—something new—then put a check with a plus sign.
(✓+)

3. If you feel anything negative, or even just an "off" feeling concerning it, then you have some resistance going on—it is a good thing when you think for yourself. Put a circle.
(O)

4. If you don't understand it—after having re-read the applicable Laws listed—that is also considered resistance. Put a circle with a question mark beside it.
(O?)

5. If you understand, but don't agree, put an X beside your circle of resistance.
(OX)

6. And if it is something you don't agree with to the extent that you resent it, put an exclamation mark next to that X.
(OX!)

7. If you agree with any showing a circle of resistance at any time, simply add a check mark.
O ✓ —O? ✓ —OX ✓ —OX! ✓

NOTE:

Please understand that these are reflections of the Laws of Truth. You may notice some may be very similar, just presented using different scenarios. That's right, they have been repeated. There is an explanation for this. Watch for it.

You will find another explanation, this one on how to assess your progress through this book, at the end of this book.

Do NOT cheat yourself by flipping forward to read it before you have finished doing the work.

Book One
PART TWO

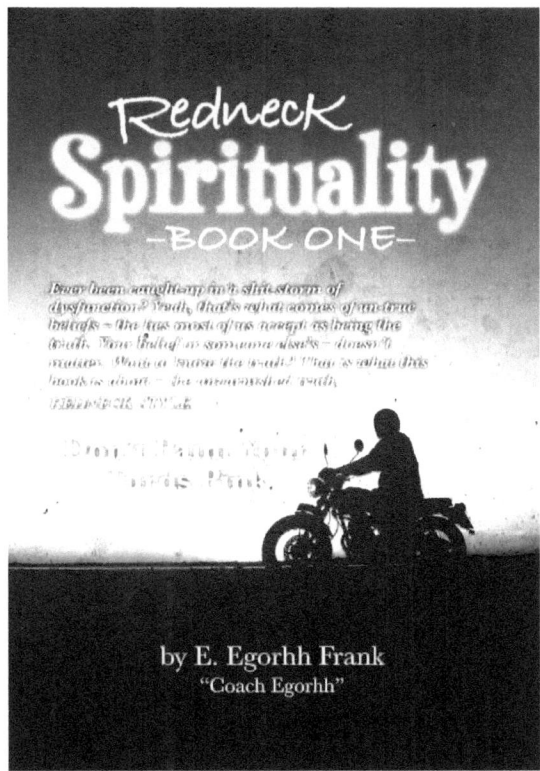

Reflections of Life
In the Light of the Laws

Peeling Onions

This book is about peeling an onion—the onion of your beliefs. In looking at the way you think about everything, you will find that *who* you are is, *what* you believe. As previously mentioned, what you believe is often based on a whole lot of lies. This book is about looking at some of those lies and replacing them with truth. Indeed, you will find it is like peeling an onion: There will always be another layer underneath to peel—and often, there will be tears.

In general, the lies come from your society—other people wanting you to live your life to suit themselves, wanting to control, and essentially enslave you. You have been taught to see yourself as a victim with other people holding the power in your life—your government, your religion, your parents, your significant others, etc.

Understanding that you are the creator of your life, and that only you hold the responsibility—the ability to respond—is your first step. These spiritual laws I have offered you in this book are the truths.

Peeling your onion will be a journey—a wondrous journey you won't regret taking, regardless of the tears. And these truths are only the beginning. You will learn about many more—and will apply the nuances of them all in your life. There is great joy in living the truth and being the master of your life.

The responsibility of holding the reins of your life is a scary thing and requires more courage than most people have. Just remember to (1) *live your life in love and not fear.* You then (2) *need no courage*, because courage requires you to first have fear. (3) *One cannot love in the space of fear*—it is one of the laws. (4) *There can be no fear if you are loving.*

I've said it four times. I hope you have taken at least one to heart. *Living in love is what brings joy to life*—there, that's five. *Don't cha just love all this oowee-goowee?* Okay, six is enough.

✶✶✶✶✶✶

See Life's Laws:
1 I am the creator.
2 Thoughts Create.
3 Thoughts are energy: Loving, or not loving (fear).
8 The world is not "out there"—it is "in here."
15 One must do one's own thinking.

Questions/exercises to consider:
- ➢ **This journey** is sometimes called "The Hero's Journey." What do you think? *Write about it.*
- ➢ **Are you** seeing some of those lies yet? Do you feel the burn? *Again, write about it.*
- ➢ **Might you** actually be enslaved by the lies? Do you want to be free—or do you think all this is all a little bit "out there?" *Yup, write about it.*
- ➢ **Can you** afford the price of not looking at it?

Omissions

Just because someone is telling me the truth—just not the full truth—does not excuse them from being a liar anywhere except in their own twisted mind. If I accept another person's lie as my own truth without searching my soul—well, that just makes me lazy and ignorant.

Regardless of my good intentions, your journey in life is your own. Don't just believe these thoughts of mine without first asking your heart. It is your heart that connects you to your soul.

I've told you nothing within this book that I don't believe to be true, and no lies of omission unless they be out of the ignorance of my own humanity—I'm searching, just like you. The fact you have this book in your hand confirms that about you. Again, my journey has lasted some 25 years. That is a lot of time to be searching one's own soul and one's world for the truth. If your search has just begun, I wish it to be as wondrous as mine has been.

✶✶✶✶✶✶

See Life's Laws:
15   One must do one's own thinking.
7   Along with being the creator comes responsibility.
2   Thoughts create.
8   The world is not "out there." It is "in here."
10   The purpose of life is for those lessons.

Questions/exercises to consider:
- **Do you** ever tell incomplete truths—leaving out defining parts that would otherwise sway your meaning?
- **Those things** your parents, your religious leaders, and society told you were the truth—did you just accept them as being true? Most everyone in the world does. Y'know?
- **Do you** believe the lies now? List every lie you now see that you have believed.

➢ **Did you** have the courage?
This question can only be answered in retrospect—after you have finished this book. Your soul always knows the truth, both the truths about life and the truths about *your* life. But few are willing to look inside. If you *work* this workbook, you will look—and you will write down what you see. Any lies you may find yourself living, will demand you change your thinking—and your life. *This is the full truth of this book—nothing left out.* Do you have the courage?

➢ **Looking at life** from the perspective of the Spiritual Laws gives understanding that cannot otherwise be seen. I will be offering that perspective in different scenarios as you progress through these pages. When you're done, I'm confident you will know exactly what the "full truth" means. Yes, the big question is one of courage. Just keep that in mind, for now. AGAIN, it can only be answered by looking back after this workbook has been worked. Answer then: *Did you have the courage?*

Pity

What if pity were just the emotional reflection of a pious mind, and had nothing whatsoever to do with compassion?

See Life's Laws:
8   The world is not "out there"—it is "in here."
3   Thoughts are energy: loving, or not loving (fear).

Questions/Exercises to Consider:
- ➢ **Yes, what** if? *Write about it.*
- ➢ **Oh, and** is there any room on your fridge door?

>>><<<

One Single Lie

There is more value in a single lie revealed than in a hundred truths. That single lie tells you where *not* to place your trust. For those given to lying, it becomes a crap-shoot, with the odds at 100% that they *will* crap-out, and tell the whole world, *"I am someone you cannot trust!"*

Problem is, most in this world are busy looking at your integrity while playing craps with their own. That's because any slips in yours is validating to their own dishonesty—thereby making it easier to live with themselves.

******

See Life's Laws:
11   Self-esteem requires integrity.
4   The energy out returns in kind.

Questions/exercises to consider:
- **What about** you? Do you place more attention on the integrity of others than on your own?
- **Once someone** has broken their integrity with you, can you ever trust them again?
- **What if** they were to admit the breach and try to clean up the mess? What then?
- **What about** your own messes? What messes have you neglected to clean up?

Actors in a Play

As a whole, humans spend most of their time engaged as actors in a play, usually a drama. We are taught from birth never to reveal our true feelings, our real selves. To do so makes us vulnerable to those who would use such information to hurt us—especially, to hurt our feelings.

Truth is, I also played those fear-based games of power, control, and manipulation. Once given the understanding of the Laws, I now choose love.

Given an understanding of integrity, I now choose friends who understand it also, and who can see it in me. Stepping off the stage—being exactly who I am—is the way to know my true friends, and them to know me.

And feelings?—I myself am the only one who holds the power over my pain. And too often, when seeing that someone I love—and thought I knew—is only an actor playing a part, I exercise that power.

******

See Life's Laws:
11   Self-esteem requires integrity.
7   Along with being the creator comes responsibility.

Questions/exercises to consider:
- **Can you** see that what we are discussing here is your façade—the pink paint?
- **Do you** see that until you step off that stage, anyone who loves you is really just loving your facade—not the real you? Is there a real you hiding behind a facade?
- **The lie** is that your facade protects you from the judgments of society. But you know your facade doesn't protect you from anything except your own feelings—don't you?
- **What don't** you think is acceptable about you?
- **What change** to your thinking will it take to muck the horse shit out of that stall?
- **Can anyone** wearing a facade ever be in integrity?

>>><<<

What Is

With those I would want to hold in close, it is not about accepting them. That's a given with everyone I know. It is merely about "what is"—about what is their integrity. In my experience of them, are they someone I would give my trust?

Given my experience of what they say they want, and the things they do—is it the same? Do their intentions match their results, *and do they seem happy with it all?*

******

See Life's Laws:
11   Self-esteem requires integrity.

Questions/exercises to consider:
- ➢ **What** besides integrity do you require to allow someone into your inner circle?
- ➢ **Do you** recognize the integrity in others?
- ➢ **Did Law 11** give you the needed insight to do so?
- ➢ **If they** aren't "happy with it all," could it be that theirs is a pretense of who they think they must be, for your approval—but aren't?

Destiny

The fact that I'm still alive means I have a destiny. I've not yet finished what I'm here to do—or learned what I'm here to learn. *AND,* I haven't yet given up the struggle.

But then, hey, who says life needs to always be a struggle? Some things I've learned along the way have been absolutely inspiring!

******

See Life's Law:
10   The purpose of life is for those lessons.

Questions/exercises to consider:
- **Do you** believe that in the pre-existence, we set goals up for ourselves to accomplish in life?
- **What goals** do you think you might have set? Which ones are yet to be accomplished?
- **Do you** believe that when we lose that innate drive to accomplish things, we soon die?
- **Is your** life a struggle, or a wondrous journey? Write about it.

Needs—Part One

My physical needs are those things I must have in order to sustain me in life. Funny thing is, my soul's needs are always about experiencing and knowing *who I am*. I have no soul needs that depend upon *others* to get filled. Oh, other people can, will, and do help me in seeing what I need to see about me. *But that is never dependent upon them changing or doing anything other than being who they are.*

Experiencing life and coming to know myself—those are the things my soul needs. Beyond my physical and soul needs, all else I may hunger for are just wants—like candy—they are not needed to sustain my life or my soul. Still, getting to that place of knowing myself completely is always a work in progress, and the true work that I—and everyone else—am here in life to do. The more work we get done, the sweeter the candy.

✶✶✶✶✶✶

See Life's Laws:
- 12   Our lives are run first by our needs, then our wants.
- 10   The purpose of life is for those lessons.
- 1   I am the creator.
- 9   Others are but a mirror for us to see ourselves.

Questions/exercises to consider:
- ➢ **List some** physical things you need for the survival of your body.
- ➢ **List some** spiritual/soul things you need for the survival of your soul/spirit.
- ➢ **Now, take** a magic marker and mark those things that require something of others that you currently are not getting.
- ➢ **Write about** how your unacceptance of them is what holds you hostage and makes you forever unfulfilled.
- ➢ **What do** you need to change in your thinking to make them acceptable?
- ➢ **Do this** exercise: Take both your index fingers and point them inward at yourself. Now say: "The correction *always* goes here."

>>><<<

Needs—Part Two

The very act of giving love to others guarantees receiving love back. It does not guarantee receiving it from those to whom it was given. When you have love for yourself, that will never be the issue. Real love is a gift. And real gifts never carry expectations.

My wife loved me the best she could, but her love carried expectations. My love, too, had its own expectations back then—the expectation of it being returned in the same manner given. I still love her—always will—but without expectations. We are no longer together—for me, she was the price of learning real love.

My love for her will always survive. It has its payback in the giving. But for a relationship to survive, love must be returned. If it is not, then the relationship is only about one or both people's fear-filled needs.

With us, it was both. We gave one another the lessons, and I learned. Did she?—I don't know. What we get from others is limited by what we are capable of receiving. I do know that I will always be grateful for what I received from her.

Very few people know what real love means. From my experience of her—now, I do. It was a true gift she gave me—though at the time, it didn't feel like it. Still, I know that the next woman I love will be loved without expectations—will her love be the same? If she lives by the Spiritual Laws, it is a sure thing.

See Life's Laws:
4   The energy out returns in kind.
13   Our own life is our sole possession. Just so, it is for everyone.

Questions/exercises to consider:
- **Have you** ever had a failed love relationship?
- **Did it** end with hard feelings on someone's part?
- **If so,** can you see how that person's *love* was only a fear-filled *need?*
- **Was that** person you?—Yep, write about it—all of it.

Needs—Part Three

The very act of giving love to others guarantees receiving love back. It does not guarantee receiving it from those to whom it was given. When you have love for yourself, that will never be the issue. Real love is a gift. And real gifts never carry expectations.

My wife loved me the best she could, but her love carried expectations. My love, too, had its own expectations back then—the expectation of it being returned in the same manner given. I still love her—always will—but without expectations. We are no longer together—for me, she was the price of learning real love.

My love for her will always survive. It has its payback in the giving. But for a relationship to survive, love must be returned. If it is not, then the relationship is only about one or both people's fear-filled needs.

With us, it was both. We gave one another the lessons, and I learned. Did she?—I don't know. What we get from others is limited by what we are capable of receiving. I do know that I will always be grateful for what I received from her.

Very few people know what real love means. From my experience of her—now, I do. It was a true gift she gave me—though at the time, it didn't feel like it. Still, I know that the next woman I love will be loved without expectations—will her love be the same? If she lives by the Spiritual Laws, it is a sure thing.

******

See Life's Laws:
4   The energy out, returns in kind.
13   Our own life is our sole possession. Just so, it is for everyone.

Questions/exercises to consider:
- **Have you** ever had a failed love relationship?
- **Did it** end with hard feelings on someone's part?
- **If so,** can you see how that person's *love* was only a fear-filled *need?*
- **Was that** person you?—Yep, write about it—all of it.

A Cry in the Dark

"If it's not love, it is a cry for love." Ah, so very true a statement! What can also be said is this: Such cries are always made in the vast darkness of fear—a place that is only dark because the ones crying refuse to turn on the light switch and face the truth about themselves

✶✶✶✶✶✶

See Life's Laws:
8   The world is not "out there"—it is "in here."
7   Along with being the creator comes responsibility.

Questions/Exercises to Consider:
- ➤ **Do you** think that those who are crying for love regard themselves as a victim in life?
- ➤ **Do you** cry for love? Or do you just give love?
- ➤ **Is it** possible that those unwilling to give love are most likely to be the ones crying for love?
- ➤ **Face it**—we have all cried for love—most do it on a regular basis. Question is: are you going to flip that light switch? *Write about the truth it would reveal.*

Bug Brains

There's life in the ride, in the cooling of sweat or freezing of nose-hairs in the wind. There's life in the bug brains on our teeth. And especially, there's life in keeping our own brains off the bumper of the next drunk we pass.

Ah yes, the *experiential* stuff of life—

There is *experiential* stuff and there is *spectator* stuff. Do spectators really live life, or does truly living require having the courage to follow one's joy regardless of the price? Are we accepting the experience of whatever comes? Most of all, do we have the courage to move past our fears?

To accept the pleasure means being willing to accept the pain equally. The universe always balances. Yes, life is about all of that. But beyond it all: The choice is bug brains on our teeth—or just in our mind's eye.

Yes, the choice is to ride, or not to ride—truly ride.

******

See Life's Laws:
14   Change is the constant of the Universe.
11   Self-esteem requires integrity.

Questions/exercises to consider:
- **Make a** list of your favorite things you like to do in your life, which are experiential. What are spectator things?
- **What spectator** things do you want to make experiential?
- **What things** do you want to do, but don't because they are too dangerous or expensive?
- **What do** you need to do to change that?
- **Will you?**

Playing It Safe

Playing life safe is the same as playing to die. To not do what one loves because it involves an element of danger is to not live.

For me, the real danger was never about something so simple as the possibility of death—rather, it was in the certainty of the price I would pay if I did not allow a loved one to run my life.

Sadly, avoiding danger is what is *normal* for most in this life. Does this mean that most in the world are just standing in line waiting to die? Seems so . . .

For me back then, it was so—but then I paid the price. The loved one is no longer in my life. And I no longer stand in that line with all those *normal* folks.

So, do you consider yourself to be *normal?* Because if you do, well, maybe it is time for you to step out of line—to truly live—to be the master of your own life. Maybe you are about to become *not normal*—like me. And yes, you will pay a price. Whatever it is, it will be worth it.

There is no safety in my life—never was. But there is self-respect—and there is joy in doing what I love.

✶✶✶✶✶✶

See Life's Laws:
13   Our own life is our sole possession. Just so, it is for everyone.
11   Self-esteem requires integrity.
3   Thoughts are energy: Loving, or not loving (fear).
4   The energy out, returns in kind.

Questions/exercises to consider:
➢ **Make a list** of the things you would love to do, but don't because it is not safe.
➢ **Which ones** are not safe because they are not acceptable to someone you love?
➢ **Which one** will you choose to do first?

Reflections of Ourselves

What I see in others is but a reflection of myself. That is the Spiritual Law.

Where it involves family, most choose to view our very worst, then blame our parents and see it only as a reflection of them. What if we were to apply the Law, only choose a better reflection?

> —To hear our own wisdom in the voice of a grandfather
> —Feel our nurturing heart through that of a grandmother
> —Know the ferocity of the love in a mother's. protective arms
> —Experience the support in a father's work-hardened hands

No, most don't look to the joy to be found in the reflection of our parents. Perhaps it is just as well. For in our pain, we find our greatest lessons. That is what pain is for.

The pain and sorrow—or the joy: One extreme comes from fear—the other, from love. The combination of it all is what makes us human. It defines the breadth of our existence, here, in this life.

******

See Life's Laws:
3   Thoughts are energy: Loving, or not loving (fear).
9   Others are but a mirror for us to see ourselves.
7   Along with being the creator comes responsibility.

Questions/Exercises to Consider:
➢ **What Positive** aspects of you do you consider as being a reflection of your parents? List them.

➢ **What negative** aspects of them do you refuse to reflect on in yourself?
➢ **What negative** aspects do you wish were not reflected by you?
➢ **At some** time in the future—after you have finished both of these workbooks—come back and answer this last question again? *Then write about it all*

A Good Day...

Did I have a good day? You bet! All my days are good days.

What do I mean? Pretty simple: It's a choice. And the alternatives—bad day or no day—really suck!

And, what about a "just okay day," you ask? Look at it this way: Is having a "just okay" life any different than having "no" life?

******

See Life's Laws:
3   Thoughts are energy: loving, or not loving (fear).
8   The world is not "out there"—it is "in here."

Questions/Exercises to Consider:
- ➢ **What kind** of day are you having today?
- ➢ **If it is** anything less than a good day, will you choose better tomorrow?
- ➢ **How** about choosing to have a *great* day every day? Write about it.

Thoughts Create

Truth is, your whole life is just the expression of how you look at it. Summed up, it is your thoughts expressed.

See Life's Laws:
8   The world is not "out there"—it is "in here."
2   Thoughts create.
3   Thoughts are energy: Loving, or not loving (fear).

Questions/Exercises to Consider:
- **Do you** want to see your life from a different perspective? If no, why not?
- **Is it** possible that because you are here reading this, the true answer is *yes?* Again—why?
- **Do you** know that not one person has ever read a self-help book while thinking his/her life was perfect?

>>><<<

We Always Know

How could I lose my self-esteem? Simple: by living outside of my integrity—by not being the same on the inside, as on the outside—by saying or doing other than I really am.

In the higher mind of my soul, I will always know. Soul uses the truth of integrity as the yardstick by which it measures and meters out self-esteem.

I can sometimes con my conscious mind into believing a lot of illogical shit. It has a huge stake in seeing me as being *in the right*, one that sometimes stretches the limits of sanity. But I can't bullshit my soul. It runs on truth—and nothing but the truth. Y'know?

******

See Life's Law:
11   Self-esteem requires integrity.

Questions/Exercises to Consider:
- **Does your** soul need a baseball bat bigger than *integrity* to tell you what you must do?
- **There are** very few people who aren't holding a big load of shit concerning the relationship between their integrity and their self-esteem. By withholding that self-esteem, their soul will rub that shit in their face. How badly does it make your life stink? *Take this one seriously and write about it.*

Integrity

Honor is not about the integrity *others* see in *me*—it's about the integrity *I* see in *me*. Integrity means that what my heart says, what I say, and what I do are all the same and held together with true intention.

Integrity is a gift given to me that only I can give. When I am in integrity, I honor myself. There is a certain integral strength in me such that I need have no heroes *out there,* for I am a hero *in here.* This is what I know. This is what others see, and it matters not if they honor it—at least not to me.

And yet honor me they will—both in respect and trust.

******

See Life's Laws:
11   Self-esteem requires integrity.
13   Our own life is our sole possession. Just so, it is for everyone.

Questions/Exercises to Consider:
> ➢ **Did you** understand the concept —*We Always Know*—the one offered prior to this one?
> ➢ **If not,** do you understand it better now? How so?

>>><<<

All that I Am

Like I once did, most folks need to tell themselves a lie or two every time they wake up, just to get themselves through the day. If they didn't—if they faced the truth—they'd have to change. And their whole life would change.

But what is the cost of not facing the truth? That cost is the price most are willing to sell their souls for, rather than to pay.

By not being honest with myself—not following my heart—I was simply lying to my soul. The extreme penalty your soul will eventually extract for lying is your life—cancer, stroke, heart disease—you get it...

For me, it was a blood clot in the lung. But then, that part is immaterial, as is my lie.

What is important is that when faced with the undeniable presence of the Angel of Death, I got real honest, real fast—and survived. Thing is, had someone explained all this to me before, would I have merely questioned his or her sanity? Would I have still denied my lies?

******

See Life's Laws:
2   Thoughts create.
14   Change is the constant of the Universe.
6   The energy of thoughts must flow.

Questions/Exercises to Consider:
- **Are you** questioning my sanity now?
- **Consciously** or unconsciously, *if* there's something you need to lie about to yourself, or a loved one—maybe even to the world—you know it. **Is there?**
- **If there** is, here are your only choices:
  1. Live your short but comfortably dishonest life.
  2. Or have the respect of your eternal soul—*Choose.*

About Changing

When the bullets are flying and bombs exploding, facing those things with courage is what most equate with heroism.

Then there are other things—like things that come so easily and naturally to a caterpillar, but require a very special kind of courage from us. Looking at what lies within and making changes is also what heroes are about.

Facing death and the unknown beyond—is there a comparison to facing life, and changing? Who you become when you change your mind, and who you become when dead to this particular lifetime, are equally irreversible. You can never go back to who you were.

******

See Life's Laws:
14   Change is the constant of the Universe.
8   The world is not "out there"—it is "in here."
15   To create a functional life requires us to do our own thinking.

Questions/Exercises to Consider:
- **Change is** such a simple thing. Why do you think it promotes such fear?
- **What is** it about your own life that you want to change? *Make a list.*
- **What change** to your thinking would be required? Make a list for each one—remember, this change cannot require anyone else to change their own thinking, or their lives, in any way.
- **In light** of *The Laws of Life,* do you get that making this change to your thinking is the critical first step—that all other steps will follow without effort or conscious thought?

Think for Yourself

What I might feast on as a delicacy, another might find repugnant in the extreme, usually because someone once told them it was. It's not about what tastes good, nurtures, or gives growth; rather, it's about prejudice.

So it always is when we don't think for ourselves. Is it any wonder humanity is so slow to change—and to grow?

We are so attached to our children seeing everything the same way we do. Like mules pulling the family cart, we pass down the same blinders we have always worn. They put them on, same as we once did—trusting us—without a thought.

******

See Life's Law:
15 To create a functional life requires us to do our own thinking.

Questions/Exercises to Consider:
- **There you** have it—the same concept presented in two different ways. Did one grab you more than the other? Why?
- **Can you** see how perception is a choice?
- **How much** of your perception is taken from the beliefs of others?
- **What might** you be missing by not thinking for yourself?
- **Now's the** time to refer to your list from the previous reflection. Did you change your thinking about anything? Do you think your family still sees you the same?
- **Is your** child wearing your blinders? *Write about that.*

>>><<<

Faulting You

How can I fault you for having the same weaknesses as I? Listen up and know: I will deal with my weaknesses. Yours are not my rightful concern.

And, I thank you for pointing out something in me that I needed to see.

******

See Life's Laws:
9   Others are but a mirror for us to see ourselves.
13   Our own life is our sole possession. Just so, it is for everyone.

Questions/Exercises to Consider:
- **What bothers** you most about the people closest to you? *Make a list.*
- **Now, with** each thing, ask yourself: "Could I ever see this in you, were it not also in me?"
- **Now ask** yourself this: "How can I place blame without taking responsibility?"
- **That** *is* what most folks do. Does it work? Do you want to continue doing it? *Write about it.*

About Limitations

We all choose our limitations. They are our security from having to be more than we think we are.

******

See Life's Law:
8   The world is not "out there"—it is "in here."

Questions/Exercises to Consider:
- **What would** your life look like if there were no limitations?
- **How many** of your limitations consist of those lies others have told you about life?
- **Are any** of them lies you have accepted, and now tell to yourself?
- **Have you** passed them on to your own children?
- **Did you** notice how this concept is like a twin to (Think For Yourself)?
- **If you** haven't already, write about all the shit from your own life that you have rubbed onto your child's.
- **Can you** smell it now?

Fools

If I think I'm a fool: *I am*—but only for thinking so poorly of myself. What other people think is really none of my business. What I know is that making it my business demands a facade.

Maybe a fool is someone who wants to know others but is too cowardly to expose his or her true self. The facade they show only speaks of the cowardly fool that they have become.

Only a fool would lie about who they are, then expect that when others like them, it is the truth.

✶✶✶✶✶✶

See Life's Laws:
2   Thoughts create.
8   The world is not "out there"—it is "in here."

Questions/Exercises to Consider:
- **Do you** show a facade to other people—it's something we've all been taught to do. Y'know?
- **If so,** how does it serve you, or does the fact you think you need it, make you a cowardly fool?—**Ouch!**
- **Do you** see that all that pink paint does is erase your real self from this world? *Write about this.*
- **Fools**—been beating the shit out of that term. Do you see how this whole facade thing we've all been taught to do is just fucking foolish? *Write down your thoughts.*

>>><<<

The Gift of Our Pain

If it is in my life, it is my creation. All emotional pain is created in my own mind, and always when it is dwelling on my past. Whether it is five seconds or five years, the event has already happened. How can it be my own creation, you ask? Why would I create such pain?

The gift of my pain is in the lesson, the "miss-take." It enables me to remember not to create the same "miss-take" again. We are simply built to succeed. We cannot succeed when we are unwilling to own our pain. We cannot succeed if we blame.

******

See Life's Laws:
7   Being the creator requires responsibility.
8   The world is not "out there"—it is "in here."
10   The purpose of life is for those lessons.

Questions/Exercises to Consider:
- **List some** of the more painful things you have going on in your life.
- **For each** thing, list the person or persons who are to blame.
- **Now consider** Law 1—yes, look it up.
- **Can you** see how it is indeed, all in your own mind?
- **Now ask** yourself this question: How fucked-up am I?
- **If you** had an answer for the above question, do you realize your "miss-take" yet? Go back two reflections to "Fools" and re-read the first sentence.

In the Face of One's Pain

Some choose to spend their lives mourning the loss of a loved one, and many view it as a loving thing. The truth is: mourning is not about love, and for most, it is a natural and healthy thing.

It is about us dealing with and moving past our pain in the fact that our lives no longer include them. Yet for some, it becomes about us using that loved one's death as an inviolable reason for not having the courage to live life as it now is.

How does one talk honestly about such an unflattering thing as cowardice in the face of one's pain? Is it so much different than cowardice in the face of one's fear? Or is it the same?

******

See Life's Laws:
8 The world is not "out there"—it is "in here."
14 Change is the constant of the Universe.

Questions/Exercises to Consider:
- **Are there** any fears in your life that you are unwilling to face?
- **Is there** any pain that you are unwilling to face?
- **Do you** know that a coward is one who won't deal with their fears or their pain?
- **Is this** you? If so, is this who you want to be?

Selfish

Are we being selfish, those of us who live our lives to suit our own wants and needs? Or is it really those who expect us to live our lives to suit theirs who are the selfish ones?

So call me selfish. To find someone who lives their "selfish" life the same way I do mine would be to treasure every moment spent *being selfish* together.

We only have this life, and the time right now to live it. It is all we are given. Why would others expect us to give it away—and even admire us for not living our lives to the fullest?

To put your life on the line—being willing to fight against those who would try to enslave you and your loved ones—yes, that is courageous. And I've got to admit: I'm proud to have done that.

Jesus died, martyred on a cross, and many see that as a holy act and sacred. I would never denigrate their beliefs. But for the rest of us, we are NOT Jesus. When there is no war—no one trying to enslave or kill our loved ones—it is just not the same sacred act, to be a martyr, giving our life for others.

Have you ever noticed how these "martyrs" take delight in climbing up on a cross, then reminding everyone of their sacrifice? Why is it so hard to see that they are really only a coward in disguise—someone who has not had the courage to live their own life? They are only on that cross because from there they get to abstain from living life, and blame it on you. And, too, from there they get to look down on you?

******

Life's See Laws:
13   Our own life is our sole possession. Just so, it is for everyone.
1   I am the creator.

Questions/Exercises to Consider:
- ➢ **Are you** seeing how the rules of society have twisted the concept of selfish into one of its greatest lies? Write about it.
- ➢ **Do you** see it as a lie to admire sacrifice as a loving, unselfish act when, at the time, there was no actual threat present?

What Is Right and Wrong

Right and wrong are not all-inclusive: What is "right" and what is "wrong" is only so in my own mind. *I* don't have the *right* to expect that others think as *I do*.

Next time you are tempted to say "Oh, that is just *so* wrong . . ." consider changing that by adding "Oh, *in my mind* that is just *so* wrong . . ."

Then—if you want to evolve—you might let go of all you consider *wrong*, and just talk about the *right*. "Oh yeah! I think that is *so* right—

And then, you might even evolve so far as to let go of *right and wrong* entirely! And just look at what is *loving—or not so loving*. That will cause you to look at yourself and who you are.

Right and wrong are your judgments of what others are doing. *But loving or not . . . Now that requires you to look at yourself and who you are being.*

Your life is really all about you—who you are being right now, and who you want to become. And that is always about being loving—or not.

******

See Life's Law:
3   Thoughts are energy: loving, or not loving (fear).

Questions/Exercises to Consider:
- **Everyone** has been taught what is right or wrong. Do you think it is the same for everyone?
- **Do you** think your rights and wrongs are solely dependent on who your teacher was?
- **Can you** see that loving is about your feelings—your energy—and not your judgments?
- **Loving or** not—what is your own choice about it? Write down your thoughts.

>>><<<

The Smallness of Our Mind

So often, we men equate sexual conquest with manliness. Why is this so? Isn't it true, it is the woman who *lets us?* She isn't conquered, she doesn't surrender—she *accepts.* Anything else would be rape.

Another equally macho fallacy, also requiring another to *"let us,"* is that if we can make another appear as *less than*, then we appear as *more than*.

In both cases, we are only displaying the smallness of our minds—and sometimes, our members.

******

See Life's Law:
16   We only control ourselves.

Questions/Exercises to Consider:
- **Come on,** guys, you do know the truth—both of them—now, don't you? *What do you think?*
- **But hey,** after a lady sees your small mind, do you really believe you can ever be a conquistador with your member?
- **Does sex** have to be a conquest with you? Do your dealings with other men require a put-down? Are you willing to open your little **macho** mind? *Yes, write about it.*
- **And maybe** this is no reflection on you. Still, it does reflect one of society's lies. Which one?—*Write.*
- **This one** is about the guys—and that doesn't mean you ladies can't express your thoughts—

The Gift In Evil

Is it possible that the "good" in good is really the gift in evil? How else can one savor all that is good in life, without having known that which is not?

******

See Life's Laws:
9 Others are but a mirror for us to see ourselves.
3 Thoughts are energy: loving, or not loving (fear).
4 The energy out returns in kind.
5 The Universe Always Balances.

Questions/Exercises to Consider:
- **Do you** see that we humans always need something to match things against, in order to consider their magnitude?
- **Do you** think it is the same with God, or whatever that higher power is, in which you may believe?
- **If your** higher power is only the good, how does "he/she/it" know anything about bad—or how bad you might be?
- **Does a** fish know air if it has only experienced water? *Write down your thoughts.*

Lessons

Our higher self—that part of all humanity which is of God—knows: The experiences in life we need for our growth will always be presented to us repeatedly until we open ourselves to the lessons. It is of those recurring happenings in our lives that we need to be especially aware. When we don't accept the lessons, they will only show up again more forcefully—more painfully—the next time.

And what is the lesson beyond the lessons? It's not God who bites us on the ass—it's our unwillingness to accept the lesson, and the gift it offers to our growth. The lesson beyond the lesson is one of appreciation.

******

See Life's Law:
10   The purpose of life is for those lessons.

Questions/Exercises to Consider:
> - **Have you** been bitten on the ass lately?—You can bet you have.
> - **If you** don't think so, then your life must be completely peaceful. Is it?

Death of a Different Sort

I think dying is just a freeing—a change in consciousness to the soul's greater awareness, and a leaving behind of one's physical body when it can no longer serve that soul. This is a standard belief.

Yet there are other deaths in life. There is the death one experiences when one leaves behind a limiting belief—is freed from the encumbrances of that belief—replacing it with one that serves. In the greater truth of that new consciousness, has the old you not died, and been left behind?

As with all death, here too is permanence: *Again, you can never go back to the life you knew*

******

See Life's Laws:
8   The world is not "out there"—it is "in here."
2   Thoughts create.

Questions/Exercises to Consider:
- **Are you** only this physical body? Or is that just the vehicle for this mind and for its every thought, every belief, every perception that you hold about yourself and your world
- **Can you** see that when you change any belief, you change the "who" you were and become someone else?
- **If it** happens that the belief you change was not one of truth, but one that limited you, can you see that you have now evolved—that the person you have become is now *more than* the person you were?
- **Would you** mourn for the person you were—who's now dead, never to return? Or would you rejoice for the person you have become?
- **All of** the above questions could be answered with a *yes* or *no*. Do you think the above concept represents thinking that is beyond the norm? Do you think it deserves answers beyond yes and no?

>>><<<

Into Her Care

A birth is a gift to a mother by the Creator—a soul given into her care and nurturing from the moment of conception. Her pain at giving birth is merely an indication, a reminder from her Creator of its worth. This sense of worth is a gift she may—or may not—pass on to the world with her loving, responsible care, teaching her child the ways of life.

The joys of her work—and its awesome responsibility—sometimes she shares with her man. Together, they leave the world a legacy. Sometimes that works out for the best—sometimes for the worst. And sometimes it is the worst that makes it work out for the best.

How I would live my life is how you must live yours. You must be the next me.

Like a job description for most parents, this is the belief each tries to instill into their child. Many parents stay on the job long after the child is an adult. Everyone has this same personal need to leave something of themselves in this world. Selfish or not, this is the standard mantra of parents from time eternal.

Will we teach our children to be our best selves, or worst? With most parents, it is both. Consciously, it doesn't much matter until comes the time for dying—and for that child to carry on.

The questions, then, to ask of their child are serious. Just how much did you grow in this life? Did I give you the same legacy as was given me? Or did I give you one better? And perhaps by my poor example, I only gave you *the chance* to be more?

Ultimately, your children create their own lives, and by the way they learned to perceive life from you, whether that is truth or lies. More than anything, I write this book for my own child, just to give him the chance by knowing that—from my sometimes poor example—*he can do his life better.*

✶✶✶✶✶✶

See Life's Law:
1   I am the creator.
2   Thoughts create.
13   Our own life is our sole possession. Just so, it is for everyone.
15   To create a functional life requires us to do our own thinking.

Questions/Exercises to Consider:
- **Given the** above questions, what legacy were you given?
  I can guarantee from experience that death always poses the important questions. How do you think your children would answer? Would you be okay if your child were to become *more* than you?
- **Could it** be that by seeing and doing life differently, they have become more, and it is you who cannot see it?
- **Do you** approve of who your child is?
- **If you** didn't teach them by the time they're eight, it's probably too late.
- **Teach them** WHAT, you ask? Try just living in the space of love.

Man's Greatest Danger

As a species, if we choose to view any animal as a threat, we will always attack. Steeped in the energy of fear, we seek to kill it first. The truth is, it is always in that endeavor wherein lies the greatest danger. For this is our *normal* response to *everything* we perceive as a threat—*including someone who merely thinks differently.*

******

See Life's Laws:
16   We only control ourselves.
13   Our own life is our sole possession. Just so, it is for everyone.

Questions/Exercises to Consider:
- **Are you** a "normal" person?
- **Do you** often rail at and demand that other people see things the same way you do?
- **What are** those things? Religion? Politics? Sex?—Or something equally irrelevant to your well-being?

My Greatest Aspiration

To know the depths of the love
my heart can hold.
To fly the rarified skies
where resides my soul.
To kindle the embers
for others with compassion.
To burn with the life fulfilling
fires of my passions.
To have the courage to abide
without fight or flight
where only love resides.

******

See Life's Laws:

3   Thoughts are energy: loving, or not loving (fear).
8   The world is not "out there"—it is "in here."

Questions/Exercises to Consider:
- ➤ **What are** your own aspirations?
- ➤ **What haven't** you done that you want to do?
- ➤ **Are you** being exactly who you want to be?
- ➤ **Have you had** any dreams that have yet to come true?—List them all.

The Sting of Truth

People will always talk. But when I get angry with what they say about me, that is when I need most to remember: The angrier I am, the more their words have carried the sting of truth.

See Life's Law:
9   Others are but a mirror for us to see ourselves.

Questions/Exercises to Consider:
- **Have you** felt that sting lately?
- Is it possible that it is your soul, giving you this same lesson, once again?
- **Whoa!** Did that one also sting?
- **Did it** sting worse this time than the last?
- **How many** more stings will it take before you die of anaphylactic shock?

>>><<<

Always

Yes, sometimes in life you must face death in order to truly live. But always! Always, you must face your fears, if you want to live with respect—your own respect!

You can live as long as you need to, without the respect of others. You cannot live long without your own. Your own respect is the response of your soul.

※※※※※※

See Life's Law:
10   The purpose of life is for those lessons.

Questions/Exercises to Consider:
- **Are there** any fears that you keep silent and secret, and refuse to face?
- **Is one** of those secret fears that others will also see you as a coward? Been there—done that too.
- **Does your** body have the ability to repair injuries and/or cure diseases?
- **What is** it, do you think, that commands your body's abilities?
- **Yes, to** cure or not to cure? Is that not the question?—the one always at your soul's discretion.

On the Line

Time? Money? Such excuses are like farts in a hurricane when it is my life on the line. Funny thing is, when it comes to being someone I can respect, my life is *always* on the line!

See Life's Law:
11   Self-esteem requires integrity.

Questions/Exercises to Consider:
- **Would you** rather die making excuses—farting into a hurricane—instead of doing the work of becoming someone you respect? *That is the work this book asks you to do.*
- **Will dying** without self-respect ever be okay with you? Been there—done that too. It wasn't okay with me. *Don't cheat yourself—write down your thoughts.*

>>><<<

About Apologies

I try to live life in the space of love—never intending harm to anyone. This does not guarantee that others won't be harmed, or at least feel they have been. Either way, I never apologize. Rather, I acknowledge their feelings and acknowledge my "mistakes" in those times when I would do something differently if faced with that situation again.

Living life in the space of love is the highest and best anyone can do, and requires no apology—ever.

Physical pain—intended or unintended—is physical, and I might unintentionally bear responsibility for its cause. But mental pain? My feelings are always my own choice and responsibility. Apologies from another only offer an opportunity for me to shirk that responsibility, which would deny me the ability to respond to my pain.

Hanging the responsibility for my feelings on another guarantees I will carry that pain indefinitely. *Taking responsibility for someone else's choice of feelings is what an apology actually is. As such, it is one of the most insidious of lies anyone can tell.*

******

See Life's Laws:
1   I am the creator.
7   Being the creator requires responsibility.
8   The world is not "out there"—it is "in here."

Questions/Exercises to Consider:
- ➤ **The next** time you think you need to apologize to someone, ask yourself, "Did I do actual physical harm to them?" If it is mental pain, then for you to take credit for it is to say, "Sure, I know you choose your own feelings, but I don't hold you capable of dealing with them—here, let me save you." Write about anything you think might validate such a statement.

- ➢ **Confused?** Go to Section One and re-read the three laws listed above in their entirety. You are now privy to one of society's greatest lies. How do you feel about this?
- ➢ **It's true** that not apologizing—not telling society's most acceptable lie—will probably lose them as your friend. The real question here is: Do you need friends who blame, then demand such a lie?
- ➢ **Unfortunately,** we live in a society that demands such lies in order for us to be acceptable. So now the question becomes: Is being acceptable worth selling your soul?

Anger

We all want to be connected. Anger is the way we often do that when we don't know how to connect with love, usually because we don't know real love. When angry, we cannot be rejected, for we have gone to that place where, out of our own fear, we have rejected them first. Fear and love are both energies—fear, being an energy that is the opposite of love, cannot co-exist.

It is an either/or choice that we make—to love or to fear. In the duality of life, there is a tipping point between *sweet* and *sour*, called *tasteless*. Just so, there is a tipping point between *love* and *fear* called *indifference*. Anger is a form of fear, and certainly one at the extreme end.

While this has already been alluded to in this book, at this point, I will give you a necessary peek into Book Two. The following is a partial quotation from law number twenty-one concerning real love: Real love begins with seeing your self-worth—and loving yourself. Until you have self-love, you have no real love to give to another.

******

See Life's Laws:
3   Thoughts are energy: loving, or not loving (fear).
4   The energy out returns in kind.

Questions/Exercises to Consider:
- **If anger** is your choice, how much of your relationship can possibly exist in the energy of love?
- **Indeed,** how much of your relationship that you perceive as love is actually fear?
- **Or is** your "love" just a fearful need to fill an emptiness—an indifferent space—within?
- **If that** person you are angry with is your significant other, isn't it likely that they are the perfect one to teach you self-love? After all, aren't they someone who sees the worth in you?

>>><<<

The Root Element of Wisdom

There is life, and there is death. Somewhere in between—if we are courageous enough to look at the truth of who we are being—there is wisdom. Could it be that "to look" is the root element of wisdom? For our "truth" and our "wisdom" are one and the same.

******

See Life's Laws:
1   I am the creator.
8   The world is not "out there"—it is "in here."

Questions/Exercises to Consider:
- **Can there** be wisdom without truth?
- **This is** your life. Do you want to know the truth of it—do you want true wisdom? Go to the *Laws of Life* in *Part One* and read the full transcript of Law 8. Now, where do you need to look for the truth? *Write about what you find. (You likely will find this to be an ongoing process. Leave room in your workbook and come back to it often.)*
- **There is** a section following *The Laws of Truth* titled, *So What's This Writer's Agenda?* In it, there is a quote from Socrates. What do you think he meant? *Write about that.*

Being "Normal"

There is so much that is of absolute magnificence concerning the human race. We share in that magnificence, for it is a part of us all—of who we are.

But, *"normal?"* Why would anyone consider that being *normal* is something to be desired? Being normal is to acutely reject all that is magnificent, in favor of *fitting in* with the socially acceptable mundane.

Doesn't this mean that being *normal* is to be the lowest common denominator of humanity? Which, too, is to say not exactly vicious, vindictive, or violent, but more importantly, it is also to say not exceptional in any positive way—and certainly, not magnificent. When does a *normal* heart ever get to soar?

******

See Life's Laws:
8   The world is not "out there"—it is "in here."
1   I am the creator.

Questions/Exercises to Consider:
- **Have you** noticed me claiming to be "not normal?" Do you now understand why?
- **Do you** now want to be able to claim the same? *Write about it.*

>>><<<

Perfect Perception

If I insist on looking for imperfection, I will always find it. Wouldn't I rather look for perfection? It is also there. After all, I am the creator of my perception, and therefore, my world. Yes, I am the one who creates my world, and then attracts what comes into it. *Imperfection—perfection:* **Which do you think I want to attract?**

The whole universe/God will jump through your hoops to make your world exactly the way you see it. If you don't like your life, don't blame God, or other people, or even the world. Rather, look to your perceptions. It is your perception of perfection that is not perfect, which brings us full circle. Your perceptions are your life, and you are their creator!

This is the hard truth. It is not some yuppie-duppie Guru bullshit! Then again, that depends upon your "perception."

✶✶✶✶✶✶

See Life's Law:
8 The world is not "out there"—it is "in here."
1 I am the creator.
2 Thoughts create

Questions/Exercises to Consider:
- ➤ **If you** are "normal," you likely had a hard time understanding this one. Did you?
- ➤ **If you** understood with perfect clarity, are you happy to be "not normal?" *Write about it.*

Count on Yourself

If you count on others, you may get short-changed. It is only when counting on yourself that you won't— if you have integrity.

See Life's Laws:
1   I am the creator.
11   Self-esteem requires integrity.
13   Our own life is our sole possession. Just so, it is for everyone
16   We only control ourselves.

Questions/Exercises to Consider:
➢ **Do you** get that without integrity, you can't even count on yourself? *Yes, write about it.*

>>><<<

Weird

We are all unique, and still, essentially the same. From the uniqueness of our thinking springs creative growth—philosophy, art, poetry, song, dance—all that which is of delight to the soul. Yet for so many, "unique" is labeled "weird" and considered a source of shame. Only those with the courage to let their uniqueness leave a mark on this world.

✶✶✶✶✶✶

See Life's Laws:
2   Thoughts create
3   Thoughts are energy: Loving, or not loving (fear).
9   Others are but a mirror for us to see ourselves.

Questions/Exercises to Consider:
- ➢ **What about** you is unique?
- ➢ **What is** just weird?
- ➢ **What will** it take for you to have the courage just to let your weird hang out?

Change Your Mind—Change Your Life

Remember Law #2—Thoughts create? How it says everything begins with a thought? Here is something else it means: *You can't change anything in your life without first changing your mind.*

✶✶✶✶✶✶

See Life's Law:
2   Thoughts create.

Questions/Exercises to Consider:
- ➤ **Do you** want to change your life?
- ➤ **To pound** these last two concepts on home: Can you see why nothing can be inviolable, nothing can be sacred, nothing can be untouchable about your current beliefs?
- ➤ **I'm not** looking for validation here. If you're going to work this workbook, write down your thoughts—agree or disagree, it doesn't matter. If you get nothing else from this book, learn to think for yourself. Those who know how are few. Do you?— *Again, write about it.*

Fearlessness of Innocence

Little children are immortal until they discover death. With the knowledge of their mortality, they learn fear. Life becomes a thing defended as they begin the process of becoming adults. The question then is: What do adults become when they rediscover the fearlessness of their innocent child—see how it is still there inside—and use it in striding along on their pathway in life? Do they then become heroes—or something more?

******

See Life's Laws:
8   The world is not "out there"—it is "in here."
3   Thoughts are energy: loving, or not loving (fear).

Questions/Exercises to Consider:
- **Ah, the** fearlessness of the immortal child—is it any different from that of the immortal soul?
- **Think about** that one. Ask yourself: Do you want to become more?
- **Are you** aware that it is only your thinking holding you back? And *THAT,* you have the power to change.
- **What would** your life be like, were you to be in touch with a little child-like fun and fearlessness? *Write about it.*

Fear

Y'know, fear can be a useful thing—it will lend flight to your feet if you have an actual tiger chomping at your actual butt.

While that may be a possibility, that sort of thing just doesn't warrant the time most folks spend living in fear and worrying, so much time that their life then becomes a fearful place.

Funny thing is, the greatest fear of all about life is death. When—Where—How—

And, *OH MY GOD! What then?* That is the greatest of the unknowns. You see, the unknown is what fear is really about.

And the worry? The worry is that we can't handle what we are going to handle.

******

See Life's Laws:
14   Change is the constant of the Universe.
3   Thoughts are energy: loving, or not loving (fear).
1   *I am the Creator.*

Questions/Exercises to Consider:
- **Is it** possible that worry is really the same thing as stupidity?
- **And fear?**—If you insist on teasing tigers, then you are right to fear. *List your fears.*
- **What do** you worry about? *List that also.*
- **How about** tigers? Are there any actual tigers prowling your life?

Standing by Your Beliefs

My strength in standing by my beliefs must always be tempered by a willingness to look at what it is I believe—to recognize just what it is about me that is served by that belief.

While my belief system guides me in life, it also limits. Growth is about releasing those beliefs that don't serve me, and adopting those that do.

Sometimes our *"strength"* in holding to our beliefs can cause us to lose that which is most precious. This process is called *"foolish pride."* Foolish pride *never* serves, for it always demands that your loved ones believe the same as you.

Making demands on another's beliefs most often begs resistance—at least from anyone who sees the "fool" in foolish.

******

See Life's Law:
8   The world is not "out there"—it is "in here."

Questions/Exercises to Consider:
- **Ah, the** "strong-mindedness" of one's forefathers: Can you see one of society's lies in there somewhere?
- **Then, how** about the unshakeable belief in one's religion? Both the beliefs of our forefathers and of our religions are sacred—inviolable. Or are they? *Write about it—all of it.*

Whole and Healed

We all walk a different path in life because we all have different needs. The parts I need to fill, or the wounds I need healed, are not the same as yours. And, we are always being offered the lessons we need to become whole and healed.

Yes, God, the Creator, the highest part of our soul, guides our personal private journey, offering the truths we need to see about ourselves—truths we don't always accept.

Those who do are the courageous ones. *Truth* is what it takes to become whole and healed. We don't tell ourselves lies out of love, y'know? Rather, out of fear—a fear called cowardice; it is only cowards who won't accept the obvious truth.

Once you look at and accept these Spiritual Laws, they are nothing short of obvious.

******

See Life's Laws:
9   Others are but a mirror for us to see ourselves.
5   The Universe Always Balances
3   Thoughts are energy: loving, or not loving (fear).

Questions/Exercises to Consider:
- **How much** of your dysfunction—your wounding—do you think is caused by the lies almost all of us were taught, and believe to be the truth?
- **How much** do you think is because we tell ourselves lies, because we don't want to accept the truth? *Explain—give specific examples—this is NOT a math lesson on unspecified percentages.*

>>><<<

Standards

Everyone must have certain standards to feel okay with themselves. Sometimes these are about things they will never allow to happen in their lives—and sometimes things they must have happen.

As for the standards of others, the yardstick for them is the same one as for you. ACTIONS! Our standards show up in the things we do, and sometimes the things we don't.

You get to create your life the way you want. After all, you are its *creator*—always. And always too, you set its *limits*. Your standards don't limit how high you fly; only how low—and who you will fly beside

******

See Life's Laws:
1   I am the creator.
13 Our own life is our sole possession. Just so, it is for everyone.
8   The world is not "out there"—it is "in here."

Questions/Exercises to Consider:
- ➤ **If you** were to raise your standards for yourself, what would that look like? *Again—specific actions.*
- ➤ **As for** the standards of others, you do know that *they* don't limit you in how high you fly—*YOU* do. *Who in your life have you been blaming for holding you back?*
- ➤ **Now about** those you have just listed above . . . *Sure, you care about them—AND, this is your life—your only life. You know what you must do. Will you give them the opportunity to live their life better by your example?*
- ➤ **By raising** your own standards, those you fly with will either be left behind or will raise their own. You don't have the right to demand that your standards be theirs. *You do know this—right?*
- ➤ *Did they* stay, or were they left behind? *Go to Part One and read the full text on Law 5—Write about it.*

▶▶▶◀◀◀

Illusions of Security

My thought system is the box that encompasses my world and provides an illusion of security. In truth, it is what limits my very being.

To increase the scope of our thought system is commendable, and sometimes even daring. But dealing with those illusions of security? —Now, that takes real courage.

You only feel secure if you think you control everything and everyone in your world. Let's look at some who thought that— Hitler—Stalin—Mao—to name a few. How well did that work for them?

Only the courageous can accept that security does not exist!

******

See Life's Laws:
8   The world is not "out there"—it is "in here."
14   Change is the constant of the Universe.

Questions/Exercises to Consider:
- ➢ **This isn't** the first time this has been mentioned. Do you accept that there is NO security in life?
- ➢ **Can you** understand why these feelings of insecurity almost guarantee you will try to control those around you?
- ➢ **Do you** think the understanding of security being an illusion might be harder for a woman to accept than for a man? One of the lies they have been taught is that they need a man for protection and security. Protection, maybe—but security? *What do you think?*

Accept

Again, when I won't accept the *"What Is's"* of my world—those I have no control over—then I guarantee myself pain. When I ignore or refuse to deal with my pain accordingly, then I guarantee myself a dysfunctional life.

When we won't accept our loved ones as being who they are, then we guarantee ourselves pain. When we insist that they change to suit ourselves, then we guarantee ourselves a dysfunctional relationship.

When you bounce through your dysfunctional life, always up in the air and using one or the other of these points to land, eventually you will run off your landing strip and crash. Then, the only question will be: "Will you survive?"

You may have noticed the pronoun used is *"you"* this time. This is because I once flew just such a dysfunctional life—and I have survived. *You, too,* can let go of all that painful dysfunction in your life. To change your life, just change your mind.

But loved ones? Loved ones simply need to be accepted exactly for who they are—loved ones. Especially when all they give in return is their fear.

******

See Life's Laws:
2   Thoughts create.
3   Thoughts are energy: loving, or not loving (fear).

Questions/Exercises to Consider:
- **Go back** and re-read the concept titled *The Gift of Our Pain*. Do you understand that the *"What Is's"* (above) are actually immortal aspects—timeless? Can you see how these concepts fit together? *Write about it.*

- ➢ **Are there** things about your loved ones you don't accept? *Explain.*
- ➢ How about those things you don't accept in life—things that you cannot control? *List them.*
- ➢ **If you've** done this exercise, likely you have quite a list. If you do, ask yourself: With my thinking this foggy, will I see the end of this landing strip before I crash?

Adults Do

Adults do what adults do . . .

As small children, we often think it is all about us and interpret those events as messages. If we should find ourselves being passed around from one adult to another, and no one seems to want us, we usually decide there must be something wrong with us—that we aren't *good or worthy* enough. If we were, wouldn't we be loved, wouldn't we be wanted?

The truth is, there's nothing wrong with the child. It is simply that some adults are unwilling to love. Small children have perfect love. They are perfect. God makes them that way—every time. But who they have been taught to be, by the time they are an adult—yeah, that can be pretty fucked-up.

✶✶✶✶✶✶

See Life's Laws:
3   Thoughts are energy: loving, or not loving (fear).
15   To create a functional life requires us to do our own thinking.
12   Our lives are run first by our needs, then our wants.

Questions/Exercises to Consider:
- **Were you** one of those fucked-over children?
- **Did you** become a fucked-up adult?
- **We arrive** in this world pristine and perfect—but does anyone ever stay that way?
- **Perhaps** it is simply that some of us need the experience of being fucked-over to grow and evolve. Did you? *Write down your thoughts about it all.*

Generations Past

Perception is a choice. Yet how much of your personal world is governed by the choices made by generations past?

We are born into a prison, built brick on brick by each of our ancestors—one without doors, but which, to sustain life, must have a few windows. Though perhaps heavily barred, and set up high, they at least let in necessities—food, water, air . . .

I think our creator provided us each a spoon with which most simply eat our gruel, completely unaware of our incarceration. Yet for the more awake few, we cherish that spoon, polish it, hold it up, and sometimes catch a reflection of the truth through those high bars—perhaps we even use it to dig our way free.

That spoon is merely the willingness to look at oneself, while ignoring the inheritance of who our ancestors said we must be. That spoon is called honesty—self-honesty.

******

See Life's Laws:
8   The world is not "out there"—it is "in here."
15   To create a functional life requires us to do our own thinking.

Questions/Exercises to Consider:
- **Do you** have that kind of honesty?
- **Is there** anything about yourself that you are unwilling to look at with honesty? *If not, explain why you are the first such person in history who does not.*
- **Don't you** know that the fact that you are reading this book says that you aren't just eating your gruel? *Explain how you feel about that.*

>>><<<

Who You Really Are

To be who you want to be requires that you express who you really are—to take the joys that are within your soul, and express them in your life.

Your soul is beautiful and complete.

See Life's Law:
8   The world is not "out there"—it is "in here."

Questions/Exercises to Consider:
- ➢ **How do** you feel about these statements?
- ➢ **Do you** understand them?
- ➢ **Do you** believe them? *Explain.*

>>><<<

Our Own Reality

Everyone lives in their own reality, and no one's perception of it is the same. I must be willing to open my mind to yours if I want to know you. Otherwise, I'll just see someone who looks like me. The funny thing is, it will be someone I won't recognize

******

See Life's Laws:
8   The world is not "out there"—it is "in here."
9   Others are but a mirror for us to see ourselves.

Questions/Exercises to Consider:
- ➢ **Given the** last concept and then this one, can you see that if you want to open your mind—see something differently—nothing can be inviolable, nothing sacred, nothing untouchable? List any beliefs you hold that you would never consider changing? *Why?*
- ➢ **What does** this say about you having an open mind?
- ➢ **Do you** understand that what you see about me, in the mirror (law 9), must *never* be ignored? *Why is that?*
- ➢ **How often** do you think that the beliefs you then see that need changing, will fit crosswise to those you listed as untouchable? Maybe—*always*? *What do you think?*

Our World

Our world *"out there"* **is in black and white: Our thinking** *"in here"* **is what colors it.**

See Life's Law:
8   The world is not "out there"—it is "in here."

Questions/Exercises to Consider:
- ➢ **Do you** color your world with the pure colors of the rainbow—the colors of love?
- ➢ **Or do** you rub that black and white into a dismal grey, or mix love's colors into an odious brown, and then flush all light with a swirl of fear, like a toilet over a black hole?
- ➢ **Two extremes**—one of love, one of fear. *Which do you choose?*

>>><<<

About Blame

Blame is just a lost opportunity to get honest with yourself—the lie you find easier to face than facing the truth.

✶✶✶✶✶✶

See Life's Laws:
2	Thoughts create.
1	I am the creator.
7	Being the creator requires responsibility.

Questions/Exercises to Consider:
- ➢ **Can you** see that in blaming others, you make them responsible—at least in your own mind?
- ➢ **In doing** that—in making them responsible for your pain—aren't you also making yourself a victim of them? And isn't that just something also in your mind?
- ➢ **Everything** begins as a thought (Law 2), remember? How does it feel to know that blaming is about being a victim—a self-made victim—one too cowardly to face the truth? *Explain.*

Being Who You Are

You have everything you can have—being who you are, right now.
To have anything more, you must become more.
To become more, you must change your mind.

✶✶✶✶✶✶

See Life's Laws:
1   I am the creator.
2   Thoughts create.

Questions/Exercises to Consider:
- **This is** one of several variations of this same theme.
- **But hey,** when one has several really great ways of saying the same thing—say them all. The person listening may only hear one. Did you hear more than one? Being a variation, did it add something or just bore you?
- **Did you** actually go back to see what I'm talking about? If not, did you answer this last question as "bored?" This question speaks to your level of participation. *Write about that.*

Right or Wrong

There is no *"right or wrong"*—except inside someone's judgmental mind. Inside a non-judgmental mind, there is only *"loving or not loving."*

Love is not something I can demand of another—not even something I can demand of myself. It is something I must *be*—if, I would know it for myself, or from another.

In the space of love, *"right or wrong"* is meaningless.

******

See Life's Laws:
3   Thoughts are energy: loving, or not loving (fear).
4   The energy out, returns in kind.
8   The world is not "out there"—it is "in here."

Questions/Exercises to Consider:
- **Did you** get that to *be love,* you cannot *be right* and you cannot *be wrong?*
- **Just** *being love?*—Have you ever been there? *Explain.*
- **Were they** to look, for many, being right has always been more important? *Did you look—and if so, were you right or were you wrong?*
- **Or better** still, *were you love?*

The Words We Use

I should do this . . . I should have done that . . .

Whenever you *"should"* on yourself, you'll always come out stinking! You see, *"should"* is another word for *"feces of the mind."* While it is usually that of someone else's mind—some faulty thinking of theirs that you accept as true. In this case, the thinking is your own. So now, let's make it personal—let's look at you.

Because words are thoughts expressed—
And thoughts create, remember—

Then the question is: Do you really want to spread all that "should" on yourself? Do you understand why you'll always come out stinking?

The *"stink"* revolves around the question of integrity. *"Should"* is about not doing something you think you need to do—your *thinking* does not match your *doing*.

******

See Life's Laws:
11   Self-esteem requires integrity.
2   Thoughts create.

Questions/Exercises to Consider:
- **Should-ing or** shitting—is either one a healthy thing for you to do on yourself?
- **In fact,** it's an odious thing to do to anyone. Don't you see, what it is saying, is: "I know better than you—I AM better than you?" *Write about it?*
- **Hell, you** must know that from the personal experience of folks who have been *shoulding* on you in your own life. How often has their shit nurtured you? *Again, write about it.*

>>><<<

Thoughts

I have everything I want—consciously or unconsciously—right now. To have anything different, I must think differently. The stuff I have that I don't think I want—that doesn't serve me—I need to search out the unconscious reason why I truly do want it, and then change that thought.

Anything—any thought—in my world that doesn't serve me in a positive manner is always a dysfunction. My thoughts create it all. My job is to create my life. And God? God's job is to bring to me anything that supports my world as I see it.

It's all good. Any dysfunction in my life is merely an opportunity to grow. My thinking is a work in progress. Were my world completely functional, I'd have nowhere to grow—Yikes! What a sad way to die.

Meanwhile, living life fully requires a certain sense of responsibility: the gut-wrenching responsibility to look at myself with honesty—to recognize and maybe even appreciate my dysfunctional thinking, *and change it.* God's job is not to correct my dysfunctions—that's mine.

******

See Life's Laws:
2   Thoughts create.
8   The world is not "out there"—it is "in here."
7   Being the creator requires responsibility.

Questions/Exercises to Consider:
- **Do you** have dysfunction in your world?
- **If you** said "NO," are you willing to consider that lie as the first dysfunction you want to address? *Address as necessary.*

- ➢ **As for** the rest of those in your circle of life, what dysfunctions do they have? Chances are, they validate your own. *What do you think?*
- ➢ **Are you** aware that in changing your thinking and releasing a dysfunction, it is likely you will also be releasing those now supporting that dysfunction in your life? *How does this one feel?*

Commitment

If you say you won't—you're honest.
If you say you can't—you're right.
If you say you'll try—you've just not got the courage to say you won't.
But if you say you will—*you'd better!*

Or else have arranged for someone who will—because you've gone and died.

See Life's Law:
11   Self-esteem requires integrity.

Questions/Exercises to Consider:
- **We're talking** integrity here. Few people really get it. Do you? *Explain.*
- **Do you** need to copy this and stick it on your fridge?

>>><<<

Death's Whisper

Sometimes the truth of life can only be heard in the surety of Death's whisper—a whisper spoken in the darkening of a night you expect will not again lighten. Death's visit always brings death. Yet for a lucky few, it is only the death of a life of lies—and when comes the light, with it comes the gift of the truth in life.

✶✶✶✶✶✶

See Life's Law:
1   I am the creator.

Questions/Exercises to Consider:
- **Does it** need to go this far before you will give yourself this gift? Or do you not see the gift?
- **Are you** afraid to look at the truth of your life?
- **I have** no room to rub your nose in this one. Death is how far it had to go before I would look at my truth. Will it be the same for you?
- **Can you** count on Death's reprieve?
- **I mentioned** earlier, this book offers you a reprieve. Do you see it yet? *Explain.*

>>><<<

A Weapon of Fear

When I can accept every person—weaknesses and all—only then can I truly appreciate the person that I am. Those "weaknesses" are merely the dysfunctions once conjured by my own soul to create the pain for change.

Evolution? Change? Is it not the same? Another person's weaknesses, when viewed in ridicule, blinds you to the judgmental person you now are. Yet if viewed in love, it can only point to who you once were, and to the magnificence of who you've become.

It's about law number three: *Our choice of energies is only love or fear.* Ridicule is but a weapon of fear wielded by you—you who don't have the courage to look at who you are.

✶✶✶✶✶✶

3 Thoughts are energy: loving, or not loving (fear).
9 Others are but a mirror for us to see ourselves.

Questions/Exercises to Consider:
- **It is** the recurring theme of this book, so again, I'll ask this question: Do you have the courage to look at who you are? If so, who is it you see? If no, why not?
- **Do you** look at and judge the weaknesses of others?
- **Do you** realize that you would not even have the ability to see those weaknesses if they are not now—or were not in the past—also within you? *Write down your thoughts.*

There in Balance

The greatest gifts life gives us are nearly always the most painful. When you are finished with choosing the pain, then look for the joy in the lesson. It is there, in balance.

******

See Life's Laws:
5   For every sorrowful thing, there exists the potential for equal joy. The Universe always balances.
10   The purpose of life is for those lessons.

Questions/Exercises to Consider:
- **Have you** ever had something almost unbearably painful happen to you, then later realized something really joyful came out of that experience? *Explain.*
- **There is** no doubt you have known such pain—everyone has. Question is: If you haven't yet, are you willing to seek out the joy? *What is your first step?*
- **If your** pain revolves around a loved one's death, do you think that person would want you to remember them with pain or with joy? *Explain*

>>><<<

It's Lies

You may change jobs, move to the far reaches of your universe, but you can never make your life work better—not until you recognize its lies. When your life stands on the foundation of a lie, it cannot be joyful—or functional.

******

See Life's Laws:
8   The world is not "out there"—it is "in here."

Questions/Exercises to Consider:
- **Have you** ever uprooted your whole life, looking to make it better somewhere else? *I did—four times. Where and when did you?*
- **What, if** anything, has changed that might cause you to stay and root out the lies next time?
- **The fact** that you are reading this book says you are searching for the truth. What specific truths have you discovered within these pages that you have or will apply to your life? *Write*

About Liars

There are just two types of liars. There are those who would look you in the eye and lie, all the while knowing it—and intending it. And then there is the rest of humanity, we who think we are honest.

I doubt there is one person alive who has not wanted to be accepted by someone he or she cared about. Cared so much so that they put on a pretense of being who they thought that person wanted.

And then carried that pretense so far that they themselves forgot it was a lie. Maybe for some, it no longer was—if that was who they, themselves, wanted to be.

But for me, there was a time when, facing death, I realized there were too many lies. So many that I no longer knew the truth about who I was. But there was one truth I could not deny, I did not like or respect this liar I found myself to be.

That's called awakening, folks. It is the first step to true honesty.'

✶✶✶✶✶✶

See Life's Laws:
11   Self-esteem requires integrity.
8   The world is not "out there"—it is "in here."

Questions/Exercises to Consider:
- **Have you** ever been there—have you taken that first step? *Write about it.*
- **Will it** take facing death for you to awaken?
  Looking at your life from the perspective of the Laws of Truth could be your awakening—if you are willing. Are you?

Endless Possibilities

The possibilities of life are endless—endless joy, or endless pain. The determining factor is: do you choose to keep your power of choice, or do you throw it away with blame?

Your choice is to live joyfully in the energy of love or in painful blame, using the energy of fear.

When I blamed, I told the world that it was that other person's fault. How many folks could see the truth? I don't know.

Few ever called me on it. But you gotta know that few were fooled. They saw me for the liar I was. So did I—and so did my soul.

So it was, I believe, that my soul sent the Angel—nothing like a little death to make a person see the truth of his or her life.

******

See Life's Laws:
3   Thoughts are energy: loving, or not loving (fear).
7   Being the creator requires responsibility.

Questions/Exercises to Consider:
- **Do you** think that lying to your soul might be cause for it to hit the reset button?

The Works of Others

Some folks manage to get quite far by claiming the good works of others as their own. In the halls of government, this is called "politics."

Those works may benefit the world, but just who are the givers, and who are the takers? Our soul is not fooled, but often our conscious mind is. It all depends on how conscious our conscious mind is of our soul.

Assuredly, a person's own gift to the world may lie in having the ability to take the ideas and expertise of others and organize them all into something of great value.

There is no shame in leadership. Leaders give credit gratefully, knowing that without the good works of others, they have nothing—they are nothing. This is the mark of a true leader.

It is only in your good works, wherein there is true joy and nurturing for your own soul, and in turn, the world.

******

See Life's Laws:
3   Thoughts are energy: loving, or not loving (fear).
2   Thoughts create.
4   The energy out, returns in kind.

Questions/Exercises to Consider:
- **What are** your own good works? *List them.*
- **If you** can't, then you need to know that no one is worthless.
- **Do you** think it's time to get to work, looking within and discovering the worth in you? *Will you?*
- **Do you** know your contribution to this world is in sharing what is inside you? *Again, will you look?*

>>><<<

No One's World Is the Same

We all live in a world of our own, comprised of every belief we hold as true. No one's world is exactly the same—the Spiritual Law, remember?

And yes. I know, I've been beating this one black and blue. But if you're still conscious, read on—

Thing is, it is where our world intersects with another's that we find a certain exquisite joy—a special oneness. Feel free to rub up against everyone you meet. Your life will be made richer. If you choose to look, you can always find some truth in their world that will expand your own.

******

See Life's Law:
8   The world is not "out there"—it is "in here."

Questions/Exercises to Consider:
- **Whose life** have you rubbed up against lately?
- **Did you** find something that enlightened your own life?
- **If you** got slapped, then you've gotta know: There's a difference between one's life and one's body. You do know that, don't you?

Taking Offense

Whenever I'm busy "taking" offense, I am giving absolutely nothing to anyone—except maybe to myself, and that would only be a bad day.

And if you're going to have a bad day, make sure the "offense" is one of physical personal security.

Emotional offenses are only taken by the emotionally insecure—the flaming victims of the world. For them, offense is the spark they strike that ignites their fearful insecurities.

******

See Life's Laws:
1   I am the creator.
7   Being the creator requires responsibility.
3   Thoughts are energy: loving, or not loving (fear).

Questions/Exercises to Consider:
- **Do you** take offense often? *How often and why?*
- **You do** know that it is the most cherished way that those who consider themselves victims have for keeping themselves that way? Don't you? *Write down your thoughts.*

Selfish Wants

Your wants *of* another are most often selfish. Your wants *for* another are most often loving. The trick is to be honest enough to know the difference—and to know when to keep your wants to yourself.

How often will a want be fulfilled when it is a demand? Demands are only made *of* another, never *for* another. A want *of* another is the one most often voiced, and also, most often denied.

******

See Life's Laws:
13   Our own life is our sole possession. Just so, it is for everyone.
16   We only control ourselves.

Questions/Exercises to Consider:
- **So, what** the fuck **DO** you want?
- **Do you** want it "of" someone, or "for" someone?
- **Or did** you get all hung up taking offense with the word "fuck?" If so, here is another law to consider: *If it is in your face, it is a lesson, a test, or a validation.*
- **This lesson** was just given in the last concept. So it must be a test, because it damned sure doesn't validate that you got that last concept. What do you think?
- **"Cheap shot?"**—Yes! But only for those flaming victims who would see it that way. *Do you?*
- **Following the** Laws of Truth, as presented here, will make you the master of your life. Don't see it? *Tell me why not.*
- **This whole** book is about me offering you the understanding of this one basic concept: *You are either a victim in your life, or the master of your life. Which do you choose?*

Conventional Thinking

If you are busy blaming others for how you feel, you are also busy trying to control them by holding them hostage to your feelings.

It is the "conventional" way of thinking. Do you wonder why there is so much sickness of the mind and dysfunction in our society? Could it be that it begins with you?

******

See Life's Laws:
7   Being the creator requires responsibility.
8   The world is not "out there"—it is "in here."
13 Our own life is our sole possession. Just so, it is for everyone.

Questions/Exercises to Consider:
- **Did you** take offense at this concept, or of the two prior—many will? If so, can you see the advantage of thinking a little more unconventionally? *Discuss it with yourself.*
- **If you** are NOT into blame, and control, and taking offense—hell, you must be just as bat-shit crazy as I. Give yourself a pat on the back—*and then write about it.*
- **In this** book are things of which many will take offense. Consider: what if that were my gift to you to see the truth of the "who" you now are—something that cannot be seen by a conventional mind? *List any truths you didn't see before, but now do because of this book.*

Wants and Demands

Your wants speak only of yourself. Be wise enough NOT to make them *demands* **of anyone, except yourself.**

******

See Life's Laws:
13   Our own life is our sole possession. Just so, it is for everyone.
16   We only control ourselves.

Questions/Exercises to Consider:
➢ **Do you** want to add this one to your fridge door too?

>>><<<

Maturity

Maturity is simply becoming secure about who you are.
The mark of a secure person is that they don't require you to change anything about yourself. They are okay enough about themselves that nothing else in the world needs change, for validation.

******

See Life's Laws:
13   Our own life is our sole possession. Just so, it is for everyone.
16   We only control ourselves.
8   The world is not "out there"—it is "in here."

Questions/Exercises to Consider:
- **Do you** ever feel the need to change other people? *C'mon. Everyone's done that.*
- **Have you** ever asked someone to agree with something you knew to be bull-shit just for the validation? *And that too. Write about it.*

Ticklish

Why is one person ticklish when another is not? Could it be that ticklish for them is simply about having a body that is set on an automatic "don't touch me mode?" Consciously or unconsciously, the mind does not want the pain it has experienced from contact with others in the past.

Then again, it could simply be the teaching of love—from loving parents tickling the laughter from their children.

Pleasure or pain—It can be so confusing when mixed on such a cellular body level.

In what other ways have you experienced pleasure being mixed with pain? Have you ever been spanked and then told it was because they loved you?

Whoa! Have you ever been spanked while making love?

******

See Life's Law:
15   To create a functional life requires us to do our own thinking.

Questions/Exercises to Consider:
- **Do you** think that ticklishness is just a physical thing?
- **Or is** it more in line with something called body or cellular memory?
- **If you** can think of other reasons for being ticklish, *list them.*
- **In the** future, when you reach out and touch someone, if tickling is optional, will you only do it in the energy of love? *(This is not about being kinky).*

The Blind Spot

Remember how Law 9 states that others are but a mirror by which we can see ourselves—that what we don't like in them is only the thing in us that we don't want to admit is there.

It's kinda like my motorcycle mirror when I'm riding. There is always a huge blind spot, dependent upon how solid my butt is planted in the saddle. The only way I can see into that spot is to get real squirrelly in that saddle—to make a deliberate effort to squirm my butt cheeks around and look.

If I don't, it's just a matter of time before that spot becomes deadly in my life. Mirrors are made for looking back and seeing things—mostly things about you. Don't you think it is time your butt cheeks got to squirming around instead of staying planted so solidly in the saddle of your ego?

※※※※※※

See Life's Laws:
9   Others are but a mirror for us to see ourselves.
10   The purpose of life is for those lessons.

Questions/Exercises to Consider:
- **While working** this book, have your butt cheeks been squirrelly?
- **If not**—well, y'gotta know: It's no fun to get run over by the semi of life. Maybe you might consider turning that ride around and cruising down this road again. *What do you think?*

Participation

These reflections are provided for your consideration, written as a personal gift—me to you. But a gift to really *be* a gift requires someone to accept it. So let's talk about how this book has been accepted in your life.

That you are still reading it this far in tells me you appreciate it on some level. Is it because it has helped you in learning the lessons of your life? Or is it just part of your search for knowledge? If so, then it is not about the lessons—rather, it is an excuse to avoid the "doing" part of learning those lessons?

Life *is* about those lessons, y'know. So let's look at your life, and just how "alive" you are living.

Your willingness to go beyond those questions that only require a "yes" or "no" answer speaks loads about your conscious participation in life. You may want to pay close attention to the questions and/or exercise part of this reflection.

******

See life's Laws:
10   The purpose of life is for those lessons.
11   Self-esteem requires integrity.
1   I am the creator.

Questions/Exercises to Consider:
- **In the** "questions" section, do you have an opinion or experience about a particular reflection that you could express, but won't, preferring to answer with a "yes" or "no"?
- **If your** "yes" or "no" answer was not the truth, do you know you are avoiding the question?

- ➤ **If it** was the truth, then doesn't you lack of explanation say you are avoiding the answer?
- ➤ **Is your** life one of what is least expected, or is it one of participation?
- ➤ **Did you** buy this book for "knowledge," or to help you change your life?
- ➤ **Does this** reflection have your hemorrhoids in a pucker?—*You may want to go back through this workbook and do the work you avoided doing.*

To Be Cherished

Sometimes in life, you get to touch a stranger in such a loving way that it makes a difference to their entire life, giving them something they could never have had without you. Sometimes they honor you for it in their heart. That is the highest award you can receive: to be cherished in someone else's heart forever—someone you did not know, and may never see again.

There was once a woman who gifted me with a ticket to a seminar here in Las Vegas. While I don't know her name, and have not seen her since, she is cherished in my heart—forever.

******

See Life's Laws:
4   The energy out returns in kind.
6   The energy of thoughts must flow.

Questions/Exercises to Consider:
- **Have you** done something for a stranger just out of the love in your heart?
- **Do you** think they cherish you for it?
- **Did you** have any expectations of them?
- **Does it** make a difference that you had nothing to gain other than giving someone your love? *Explain all of the above.*

Being Authentic

Worrying about how others see you will prevent you from being authentic—*EVERY TIME*.

******

See Life's Law:
13   Our own life is our sole possession. Just so, it is for everyone.

Questions/Exercises to Consider:
- **Are you** one of those who worry? Why is that?
- **Do you** know that what others think is personal—and none of your business?
- **Will you** stop worrying?—The keyword here is "will." It is not "can."
- **Isn't all** that pink paint getting expensive? Write about what the cost is to you.

>>><<<

The Last Haunt

I have known the bony embrace of the Angel of Death, and had so much then that haunted me. And since, under that piercing stare, I have come to witness the true magnificence of life.

And now . . .

A few remembrances—a few sweet songs—and let the ashes fall to the winds and the canyons of Southeastern Utah, my final homeland. However that last goodbye goes, the best I can wish for is that someone remembers some spark of my life I might have shared, and kindles it anew in their own—and then passes it on.

Ah, to raise the energy of the world just a little—for the single question that haunts me now in considering my going is: *Did I give as much as I took?*

Perhaps this book will kindle a spark for you—perhaps you, will do the giving for me.

******

See Life's Laws:
3   Thoughts are energy: loving, or not loving (fear).
6   The energy of thoughts must flow.

Questions/Exercises to Consider:
- **Do you** think it has kindled a spark—or will? And of what would that be?
- **Have *you*** given as much in this life as you've taken? Will this book help in that endeavor?
- **Death *will*** come for you, and you don't know when. Did this book give you answers about your life now—answers you will want to know then?

>>><<<

Epilogue

As the title suggests:
Don't paint your turds pink—don't put the lie to the truth that has nurtured the "who" you are. Most have been slopping that pink paint around so long that if they ever did know the truth, it has been forgotten. My hope is that you've used this book to search out the "who" you are beneath that paint. You will find there is nothing you'll want to cover—and no stink to embarrass you. There's only beauty—such beauty as would rival the most exotic of butterflies.

THAT . . . is who you are! That is who we all are. My most endearing wish is that we would all choose to look for, and find that beauty, even if but for a brief glimpse. That glimpse will transform your life. If, through my own stumbling redneck efforts in writing this book, you may catch that glimpse—hell, my life might then have made a difference. And so I say this final thing one more time—but differently. If you haven't yet, I hope you now will hear it.

As the spiritual law states, **Thoughts create.** The truth of who you see yourself to be IS who you are being. Are you a crawling larva, or are you that butterfly? Your soul is that butterfly—and more. In this life, your thinking is what limits you. You are here to grow your thinking.

In the end, the Angel of Death comes for us all. Question is: Will you be the butterfly?

>>><<<

The Assessment

Go back through your workbook and reassess those things you marked with a circle of resistance. If you find you no longer feel that resistance, then ***put a check mark next to it.***

These workbooks are not about being *right* or *wrong*. This book is *only* about seeing the workings of *The Laws of Truth* in your life. It does not have to be the same for *you* as it is for me. The point of this book is to give you some real truth —*the Laws*— and then **to get you to look within yourself**.

This assessment is to tell you if it did that, and if there has been any change in your thinking. If there has, then this book has been instrumental in changing your life.

Change your mind, change your life.

And, there is one further thing this book is meant to show you about yourself. Go back through it and note whether you still have any circles of resistance with resentment not yet checked off.

(OX!)

If there are, then I would coach you to get and do *Book Two*. There is another assessment in the back of that book.

AGAIN, do NOT cheat yourself by reading that assessment before you have also done the work in that book.

One Last Thing

There is a concept titled "Participation" near the end of this book wherein you were asked to take note of those in the question sections that could be answered with a simple *yes* or *no,* and to look at your level of participation—did your participation end with a yes or no answer? Book Two is the next level in your participation. It is NOT by way of a sales pitch that I say this. This is currently a two-book series. Book two is more advanced in its concepts, covering much that book one does not. To give you a small taste, there are an additional ten laws, one of which is as follows:

Law 26—Change requires truth.

You cannot change anything about your thinking unless it is the truth about what your heart wants. And you cannot change anything about your life without first changing your thinking. Change your mind, change your life. (Yeah, it is a law). Pretending to accept someone else's thinking is to live a pretend life—never sustainable, always dysfunctional.

* * *

If on one of those *yes* or *no* questions you realized that you had something dysfunctional going but you simply didn't care enough to change it—fine. You cannot make changes your heart doesn't want.

Simple—yes! And, you may want to go back over those *yes* and *no* answers and consider the ramifications of your lack of participation. Are you cheating yourself out of realizing the consequences of that dysfunction—by not becoming fully aware?

A Redneck Example:

What if you have always farted whenever you felt the urge. Barring wet surprises, that has always been functional for you. But hey, when you fart in public, that energy may not feel loving or functional to others—especially in places like elevators.

Others in that elevator are going to find you extremely unacceptable and consequently will stay away, just as soon as the door opens on the next floor. *Now* you realize why you have so few friends. *Now* you see the dysfunction and have a reason to care enough to want to change. *Now you can and will change.*

***That change is now sustainable because you are making it for you*—** Law #26, remember.

> ➢ **As a final exercise** for this book, go back over **every** question that pointed out a dysfunction about you, or your thinking—those that you did not think warranted further thought or action. Consider what the true consequences may be to your life. Use the blank left side pages in your notebook to write about what you now see.

This might be your most difficult exercise. It requires brutal honesty and is meant to give you an indication of what stinks in the elevator of your life.

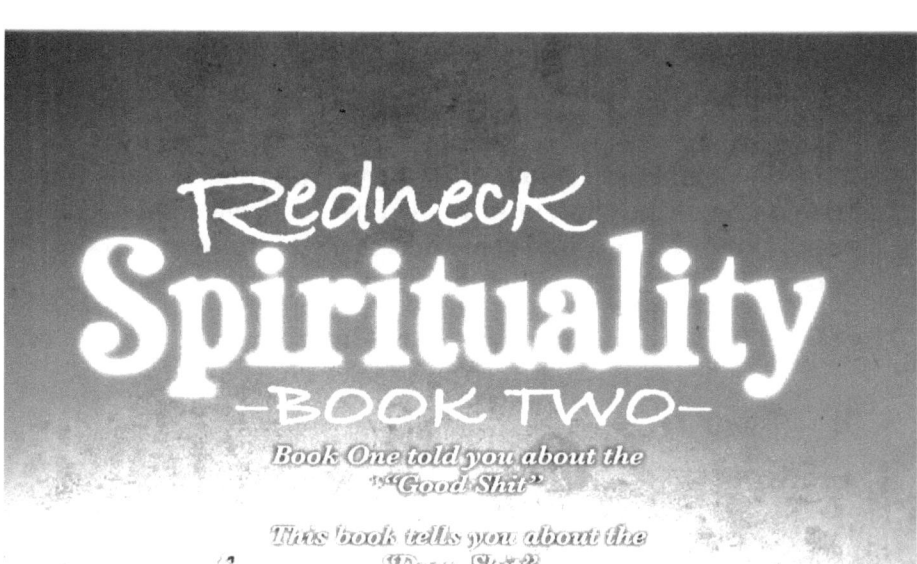

If Shit's In Your Face
　　　Somethings Stinkin'
　　　　　In Your Thinkin'

Please Note:

In this, the combined version of Redneck Spirituality books one and two, some of the content in Book Two has been removed. The stand-alone versions had some necessary redundancy in the materials presented, which in this edition is unnecessary.

The layout is also re-ordered somewhat in order to streamline the number of pages.

Dedication

To my big brother Mark,
who never saw how the pain
of a seven-year-old being thrown away,
was what ran his insanely dangerous life—
right up until the gunfight that ended it.

You had nothing to prove to me,
and the truth was,
there was no one left,
but you and me.

I loved you then—
I love you now—
But I could not save you.

Only you could slay
the dragons of your mind.

Epitaph

Governments attempt to control

by force of arms—

societies and religions,

by force of mind.

You may not be aware,

but both forces are actively

controlling you right now.

What it takes to be free

IS TRUTH.

Cliché though it might be:

the truth will set you free.

This book is about that truth.

                                              Coach Egorhh

Acknowledgments

To the Sin City writers' meet-up group for all their great critiques. And to Bobby Daniels Graphics, who did excellent work on the cover.

Thanks go to Dee Ann Leger and Karen Diehl for their excellent editing.

It was great to have such supportive people behind my efforts in putting out this work. Couldn't have done it without cha . . .

Thank you, thank you!

Egorhh

Introduction

If you want this book to tell a story and entertain you—it doesn't and it won't. If that is all you feel you want, read a book called "Peter Pan." It's a wonderful fairy tale—not so this book.

This book is no fantasy. It is about transforming your life—about making it more functional and peaceful. However, there are many who would have no life if they weren't kicking up a little drama to provide excitement. If this is you, then this may *not* be the book for you—unless you would like to replace all that drama with some healthy excitement.

As the author, I need to explain that I've always lived life as a redneck. As stated on the cover of Book One, what that means to me is that my life has always been lived on the cusp of crudity. As such, "Redneck" is the language—the crudity—with which I am most comfortable speaking. However, outside of a little crudity, I will endeavor to limit myself to good, clear English in the following reflections. After all, they are the reflections of what it means to live life under the Spiritual Laws. I would be negligent if I did not do my best to aid you in understanding them. And please understand also that some things I feel are best spoken in Redneck.

If you are one who ***doesn't*** like crudity and ***will*** take offense with it—well, feel free to do that ***now***. Don't get your hemorrhoids all in a pucker by reading this book.

While it is not my intention to offend anyone, there are those who never miss an opportunity to take offense. I didn't write this book for them, but rather for you, who will cherish and appreciate what this book adds to your life—you, the open-minded ones.

The Spiritual Laws are the Laws of Truth—and I have the utmost respect for the truth. That is because, like nearly everyone alive, I too was taught the lies. Yet few ever see them until the dysfunctional results have reduced their life to ashes. That is the place from which—like a Phoenix—one then needs to rise, a place where some start looking for the truth. Not so for me. For me, it was The Grim Reaper—The Angel of Death—or rather, his presence that sent me searching.

You see, I injured my leg and had a massive pulmonary embolism—a blood clot—in my lungs. I was not expected to live.

In the presence of death, how could I continue with my life's lies? I saw clearly how my whole life was one of pretending to be who others wanted.

At first, the "good Mormon son" my parents wanted, and later, the "limp-dick controllable husband" my wife wanted.

Yes, I pretended so long that I forgot who I was—but knew I was someone I didn't like or respect. How could I accept death when it was so clear that I'd never lived a life I could honestly call my own?

And so it was that the angel took pity—gave me a reprieve—the time needed to search out the truth about life, and about me. That was 25 years ago.

That truth is what this book is about.

Will it be the same for you? Will you see your own life's lies when The Angel comes for you? Maybe you'll double down, insisting that your life has no lies—not a good bet.

My bet is that you will want to know the truth. You KNOW that at some unknown time, The Angel WILL come. And too, you gotta know—he gives very few reprieves.

As mentioned in Book One
you might consider this book series
to be your own reprieve—
passed from the Angel,
through me,
to you.

Book Two
PART ONE

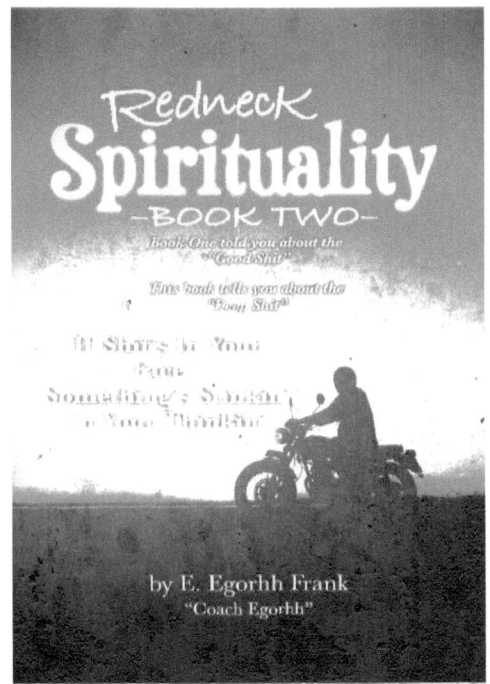

Life's Laws
The Truths of Life

About the Laws

The following truths governing life are what some would rather call "Spiritual Laws." I prefer the term Laws of Life. For many, "spiritual" is another way of saying "religious." And this book is not about religion—certainly not "organized" religion. But it does include the concept of a Higher Power—a concept that does not require religion.

A note here for those who, like myself, are likely to get their sphincter all bound up over the linguistics of calling these "Laws." Feel free to call them "Principles" or "Truisms"—or any other word you choose. It is not I who calls them laws, it is life that calls them so. Like gravity, they "just are." If you don't observe the Law of Gravity, it is your body that gets the broken bones. Don't observe these Laws of Truth and your life gets the broken bones—they are the "dysfunctions" upon which you hobble through life.

In Books One and Two, the focus is on truth. As mentioned, we have all been taught a boatload of lies with which we are expected to run our lives. This book does not specifically divulge what those lies are. By telling you the following truths, I expect you will be able to see them. Living by those lies always guarantees dysfunction in your life. To change any of it, requires the truth.

We are all built to be right. Being right is the glue that holds our lives together (more on that later). For now, let's just say that there are those who don't have the ability within the paradigm of their thinking to see, much less move past the lies.

For them to understand these concepts, Book Three may be a necessity. Problem is, I am not into stroking anyone's resistance. Besides, how does one write a positive book dealing with negativity? And, some say that is exactly what Books One and Two do—you decide.

It is entirely up to you if you want to believe what is offered in this book. It is just that with so many folks hobbling around on their dysfunctions, they are going to stagger into your life. Do you want to put up with their shit? Accept these truths, and you will see it coming before it has slimed you.

It has been said that nothing is all black and white—that there are no absolutes. They are not talking about the truth. The truth is always an
absolute. The laws are the truth. Base your life on these truths and it will ALWAYS be functional. But base it on those lies. . . .

These laws have always been around. And you may well have come across them written by others using other words. Likely you too, never understood their depth of meaning. *That* only shows up by living them—which few do. *That* is what this book is meant to do—to illustrate them in action. *That* is my gift to you. Something I received, at the cost of everything I once held dear, but now offer you without expectations. Accept this gift —or not. Again, it is up to you.

In receiving it, will you too pay a price? Yes, likely so. And from experience, I guarantee, whatever the price, *it will be worth it.* (More on that later).

A bit melodramatic? Maybe. Still, no matter where you are in the order of all this, that you have this book in your hands says your soul believes there is something here for you. For it is your soul that in every moment of life, is providing the lessons you need.

This is your life, and you are its sole creator . . .

A deep water river often provides a smooth surface. No matter how clear the water may be, given that it is deep, likely you will not see to the bottom. If the following laws do not seem all that interesting, it's okay. The reflections of the laws that follow in the rest of this book should provide you with what you need to see. Looking at life through the truth in these laws provides a very different view—a view you have likely never seen. Seeing what is beneath the surface here, hopefully, will intrigue you.

To aid you in understanding, the applicable laws are listed with each reflection.

The Laws of Life

While the first 16 have already been listed in the "Book One" section of this combined volume, they are reprinted here for your ease of reference.

1—I am the Creator.
Most only take this to mean I create my own life. That is true. But to own it requires me to understand that there is nothing in my life that I have not had the deciding factor in creating. It is true, too, that all other Spiritual Laws presented here are just aspects of this one. As you read through and comprehend the concepts in this book, you will get a sense of how this Law touches upon the infinite. This is your life, and these are its truths.

2—Thoughts create.
Look around you. Everything our species ever created began as a thought in someone's mind. As for the rest, there is an order to the universe. One that speaks to sentience—to feeling, sensing, understanding, creating—like us, but much more. It is a "Higher Power" infinitely beyond what our religions can conceive.

3—Thoughts are energy.
In being our own Creator, we choose in every second of life, the energy with which we are creating. It can only be one of two energies—the energy of ***all that is love***, or the energy of ***all*** that is not love (fear).

4—The energy out returns in kind.
The energy of your every thought determines what comes to you in life—*love* or *fear*. This is that freedom of choice which is our greatest gift of all Creation. It is this choice that creates the path of our lives and the quality with which we walk.

5—The Universe always balances.
With every sorrowful thing, there is the potential for an equal joy, yet we are the creators in our lives. There is equal joy to be found in every sorrowful event *if* we will look for *and* accept it. The truth is, it is we who have chosen the sorrow, and it is we who must seek and choose the joy. The potential for both exists in balance within the universe, and we are but a shift of mind away, requiring no more struggle than the acceptance of our next breath.

6—The energy of thoughts must flow.
Once taken in, the energy of fear stays and is the initial cause of all sickness *if* it is not felt, acknowledged, and then released. Even love energy must be released—given back out—in order to flow.

7—Along with being the creator comes responsibility—one cannot BE the Creator and play the blame game.
One cannot *not* create. Each person must accept responsibility for the totality of creating their life, especially for all thoughts and feelings associated with that process. **Blame is the abdication of responsibility, the greatest of all Mankind's dysfunctional lies.**

8—The world is not "out there"—it is "in here."
It is comprised of every thought, every belief, and every feeling you have. Your world is totally your responsibility because you are the only one who has the ability to respond—the ability to make it better or worse, loving or fearful. **Only you can change your mind.**

9—Others are but a mirror for us to see ourselves.
What we don't like in others is but the reflection of what we don't like in ourselves. If it were not also within us, we could never see it in them.

10—The purpose of life is for those lessons.
When we refuse the learning, the lessons will be presented again, more forcefully, until we learn them—or die.

11—Self-esteem requires integrity—it is the respect of your soul.
What our heart feels, what we think, say, and do—all must align as the same, and be coupled with the strength of intention to be in integrity. Integrity commands esteem.

12—Our lives are run primarily by our needs, then by our wants.
As such, our lives are mostly run from an unconscious level. We all know what it is we want—few know what we need to have it. Needs are about the necessities—wants are about the quality.

13—Our life is our sole possession—and so it is for everyone.
We, being the Creator, have all the say in creating our own life—no say in the creation of anyone else's. They are always free to be, say, or do whatever they want—without actual harm to others.

14—Change is the constant of the universe.
Change is fearful. With everything we find fearful, change—the unknown—will be at its core. Fear? Fear is *not* a constant. It is a choice (Law 3). And sometimes, it is a barometer for change.

15—To create a functional life requires one to do one's own thinking.
The beliefs passed down through the generations, as well as by our religions, are generally accepted as truth. Even when those "truths" serve us falsely, few have the courage to think for themselves. It takes great courage to think differently in the face of family and/or religion.
Dysfunction will always come when living the lies passed down to you by others.

16—Controlling anything outside ourselves is a fallacy.
We can only control another inasmuch as they will let us—or rather, pretend to let us. And our world? See Law 8. Yes, we control our own world, because it lies within us.

17—The energy to which we hold fast is what runs our lives.
Mostly, it happens from an unconscious level. This is why on the conscious level, forgiveness is so important to our souls. Forgiveness means, to let go of that energy.

18—Soul-to-soul pacts are made in the pre-existence.
Each agrees to provide the lessons in life that the other needs for the growth of their soul. Those people in your life who it seemed were especially mean—maybe you asked them to be. Was there a lesson from them that required them to be so?

19—We are quintessentially beings of energy.
Our energy affects that of others around us. We cannot avoid it and are always attracted to those of like energy.

20—God the Creator—that Higher Power—infuses the energy of the whole universe.
We are part of that energy—we each are a part and piece of God.

21—Real love, once given, cannot be taken back.
There are all kinds of interactions that are generally billed as "love"—lust, caring, companionship, even ownership. All that mislabeling notwithstanding, "real love" is an all-or-nothing gift, given without exceptions, expectations, or demands for anything in return. Real love begins with loving yourself. The love you hold within you—for you—*is* the love you give to another.

22—We can only feel our own feelings on a conscious level.
Your love for another is a gift you give to yourself. As for the feelings—the energy—of others? That is felt at a higher unconscious part of our Souls. Our Soul comprises the total energy of our being, most of which is beyond the conscious. On this conscious level, you can only feel yourself loving them.

23—All life happens right now—now is the only time there is for the living.
The past is dead, and the future belongs to our dreams. We have only
"THE NOW."

24—Whatever our thoughts dwell upon with energy, is what we are attracting—right now.
It may be our fondest dream—or our worst nightmare. Some call this ***The Law of Attraction.*** It is simply how we use our energy in the creation of our lives.

25—Your every word is an order to your soul.
Thoughts create, and if you don't want them manifested into your life, then that thought, and especially every thought once spoken, must be consciously cancelled, **with passion.**

26---Change requires truth.
One cannot change anything about one's thinking unless it is the truth about what one's heart wants. And one cannot change anything about one's life without first changing one's thinking. Change your mind—change your life. Pretending to accept someone else's thinking is to live a pretend life—never sustainable, always dysfunctional.

The Bottom Line

Y'know, it's hard to be a fresh voice writing about Spiritual Laws and concepts that have been around all through the ages. Even the ancient Greek philosopher, Socrates, talked about them.

"The unexamined life is not worth living."—Socrates

Examining and understanding who you are and what your true responsibilities are in life is the crux of these Laws of Life. While there are other Spiritual Laws that touch on other matters, the ones listed in this book series all concentrate on your responsibilities in life.

Fresh? Different? What does this book series have to offer that all those before it didn't? Perhaps it is the fact that in the past, there have been few writers with the cajones to say it like it is. It would be so much easier and more profitable to give you a feelie-good workbook.

This is NOT a feelie-good workbook!

For many, were it to be written in terms that make it feel good, it would only validate their existing dysfunctional thinking and change nothing. The things you need to look at, that can and do change your life, are those things that DON'T feel good. The truth of these Spiritual Laws does not depend upon your acceptance. If you are living a lie, seeing the truth will always be uncomfortable because it demands change—change never feels good until after it has become familiar. So decide now if you want it. Living a dysfunctional life may not be all that enjoyable, but it does feel safer than making changes. So now, let's talk about the lies.

It is not "politically correct" to tell you just how badly your life has been "anal-lyzed." Shit! Those dysfunctional lies you have been taught upon which you "should" base your life—it might help to know that *"should" is merely the shit from between someone else's ears.*

But hey, that is just the human condition. A smell is just a smell—we are the ones who say when shit stinks. Face it: no one finds the smell of their own shit all that repulsive—well, do you? If you did, it would make it difficult to live with yourself—now, wouldn't it? It is only other people's shit we think stinks—no matter out of which end it comes.

Politics be damned! It also begs acknowledging—clearly—just who those liars are that wiped all that "should" off onto your life. They are your *parents,* your *religions—all those whom you love and respect.* Why else would you just accept those lies without question? Just know, it was never a deliberate thing. They accepted it all before you, same as you. Consider: what if the person telling you all that "should" had been someone you didn't even know—some redneck, maybe like me?

Yes, puts it all in a different light—doesn't it? I encourage you to think for yourself, and to question every word you read in these pages, and everything you are told from now on—forever! This is what it takes to be free—for your thoughts to be truly your own.

And the "shoulds" that lie between your own ears—are they indeed, your own? Do they uplift and nourish you with truth? The thing about shit is that it is about what has nourished you. What makes it stink so badly is when it has never nourished you, likely because it came from between someone else's ears. Instead of nourishing, it has made you a stinking victim in life.

To be honest, didn't I just tell you how *your life has been* "anal-lyzed"—how you have been a "stinking victim?"

Whoa, hey! Have I also been "should-ing" on you?—or am I offering you a choice?

The key words here are *"your life has been."*—PAST TENSE!

Point is, that was the truth about your past. It is now up to you if that will be the truth in your future. Within the cocoon of these Spiritual Laws, that victimized pupa from your past now has a chance to become a butterfly.

And me?—What do I get for rubbing all this truth in your face? I fully expect *some* will want to crucify me. Hell, Socrates was put to death for this same act of politically incorrect social disobedience.

My purpose in exposing you to these truths is simply to offer you an opportunity to make your world—and mine—a little better place. I have no desire to be a Preacher or Guru. I'm just tired of seeing this shit-storm of dysfunction swirling all around—and knowing the reasons behind it all—and yet not caring enough to open my mouth and risk condemnation. Twenty-five years ago, The Angel gave me a reprieve. This book series just may be his reason.

This is not a big book, but if you're paying attention, it will be a long read. Take your time.

It is meant to be a workbook. Whether it is a hard copy or digital, it doesn't matter. To work it, you will need a notebook, preferably one that is a binder. At some point, you may need more space and want to add a page here or there. In the beginning, write only on the right-hand page. The reason for this will be explained later. Write down the title and page number of the reflection, then answer the questions and do the exercises.

How much this book will add to your life will be determined by how much work you are willing to put into it. Some will buy this book and read it for the information. They want knowledge—they don't want change. That is okay. For those who do want change, the writing is the easy part. I guarantee that if you work it, your life will be different—better.

And, just maybe, you will want to make a difference for someone else—perhaps even one of those liars whom you love. Without you, they likely will never have a clue about those lies. Pass this book on, or better yet, buy another and pass that one on. The debt everyone owes to that Higher Power for the privilege of being alive *is to live a life that makes a difference.*

Could be that—like me—*now's your chance . . .*

>>><<<

To Set You Up To Win

As explained, *Book One* has sixteen of the Laws listed. This book has expanded that to twenty-six, and includes aspects of *love and love-relationships,* as well as the really dangerous shit to consider: *organized religions, God, spirituality, and—oh my God—politics (always cheesy shit).*

Just remember: I am not telling you what to think. You decide that. But it is a moot point if you decide *not* to think. If that is your choice, then it is pretty much a given that the energy you are deciding with is *not* loving. You see, I am merely asking you to consider *how* you think—what is the energy in which you think? If you accept the truth in Law 4, it states that there are only two energies: love or fear. This book is written in the energy of *love.* When reading it, I ask you to think for yourself, but you think in the energy of *love*, not *fear.*

All "organized religions" work through the energy of fear. The fear of what that Higher Power they claim as their authority—God—Allah—Hari Krishna—etc—might do if you disobey. And too, the fear that your connection with that Higher Power rests solely with them. You get the point?

Yes, I told you this is NOT a feelie-good workbook!

Then, there is love and loving relationships—love is where a lot of thinking really gets to stinking—and where a lot of folks get out the pink paint. What those involved may think is love, those not involved can see it for what it is—not love, but fear.

So, if in the process of reading this book, your cheese starts sliding off of your cracker—let it. You may find you then have an opportunity to take a breath of fresh air. Your cheese has been moldering and fermenting in all that fear, and you no longer notice the stink. It may be the only way your soul has of showing you how badly your cheese stinks.

Your soul is the part of that Higher Power charged with showing you the things you need to see—or rather, the lessons you need to learn in this life. No doubt there will be some things in this book that won't feel good. Is it possible that pointing those things out is why your soul put it in your hands in the first place?

Book Two
PART TWO

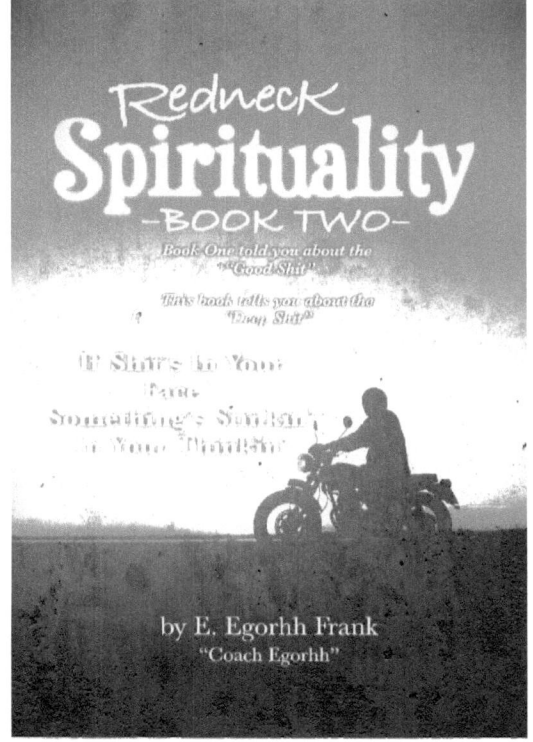

Reflections of Life
In the Light of the Laws

The Wonderment

Until you've looked inside yourself,

you'll never know the wonderment,

of knowing just what you can do,

of seeing who you really are.

The depths of your courage . . .

The breadth of your heart . . .

The heights to which

your soul can soar . . .

With so much magnificence to discover,

why would you not want to find?

When only stopping you are your fears . . .

the imaginary dragons of your mind.

My Shit Don't Stink

As mentioned in the beginning section of this book (in The Bottom Line), let's talk about shit—or rather the stink of it. Have you ever noticed how, when two dogs meet, the first thing they do is stick their nose into the other dog's ass? The reason is simple: They don't have sweat glands in their skin, and so they smell each other's ass in order to be able to recognize one another's scent. They don't judge if the other's butt smells good or bad—a smell is just a smell. Any judgment they make has already been made. By reading the other's demeanor, they already know if that other dog is loving or unloving—a danger, or not a danger—and have decided to get acquainted.

We humans are supposed to be the advanced species. Why is it we aren't that smart? Why do we judge everything about one another as good or bad? Why is the smell of our own shit acceptable, while the smell of another's is not? For us, smelling one another's butt is unnecessary. Even so, we too have eyes and can see. We too only need to judge if the other is loving or unloving—a danger, or not a danger—someone we want to know or not.

If you own dogs, you know that you are part of their pack—hopefully their leader. If a dog has any fault, it would be its loyalty. When faced with unconditional love, we humans seldom respond with love. When we have no love within ourselves, we have none for another. Within our own species, it is seldom that we encounter unconditional love. It is the fault of our teachers who confuse us with the idea that we must love others, while negating the idea of loving ourselves. How insane is that?

******

See Life's Laws:
3   Thoughts are energy: Loving, or not loving (fear).
4   The energy out, returns in kind.
8   The world is not "out there"—it is "in here."
1   I am the creator.

Questions and/or Exercises:
- **What does** all this tell you? In fact, what's it all about—what is the underlying thought here?
- **Is it about** the stink of shit?
- **Is it about** judging things good or bad?
- **Is it about** the behavior of dogs?
- **Is it about** the energy we choose to live within—loving or not loving?
- **About some** things, our species is down-right fucking stupid. What are those things?
- **You may** come back and answer this last question after completing the rest of this book

About Pink Paint

It's been mentioned how our society demands we paint our humanity with the pink paint of "a gentleman" or "a lady"—that we must wear a facade—because if others could see who we really are, we would not be acceptable.

But making ourselves out to be fakes and frauds is but one of society's dishonest demands. There are many other lies we have been pressed to believe, and on which to base our thinking—indeed, our very lives. Many of those other lies were taught by our parents, our friends, our teachers----and oh yes, especially by our religions.

We have been taught so many lies that our lives have come to revolve around a game—a game called *blame*. Blame and control, instead of love, our relationships now consist of little more than playing that game.

The Reflections offered in these workbooks are about showing you life from the viewpoint of truth, as reflected by the Laws of Life. The first, and most important law is that you are the creator of your life—it designates your responsibility in life—and means basically, that "blame" can no longer be in your vocabulary. Without blame, you need no control over others.

******

See Life's Laws:
3   Thoughts are energy: Loving, or not loving (fear).
4   The energy out returns in kind.
8   The world is not "out there"—it is "in here."

Questions and/or Exercises:
- **We all** have our own traits that make us human. What are yours?
- **Can anyone** really accept you—indeed, know you—if you hide those traits?
- **Do you** see yourself as a loving individual? Why?

- ➤ **How much** of your relationship with your significant other is about blame and the struggle to control? The next time you find yourself in a "lover's spat," ask yourself that question.
- ➤ **Surely you** can see how fucked-up the pink paint of a facade really is? —In fact, how fucked-up are all the lies that you have been taught?
- ➤ *The main exercise of this book is now to write down the lies as they become obvious to you. Use the blank left side paper in your notebook/binder and put it next to whatever reflection you are currently writing about.*

Admission Price

Making someone unacceptable is always about playing the game of control. It is about me, demanding you change something about yourself—that being, the price of my acceptance. What I don't see is that I am only buying your pretense. What *you* don't see is that whatever the demand—whatever my price—you are being cheated.

For my acceptance? It also, is only a pretense. And the real price we both pay is one of honor. No one plays this game unless they are holding the other responsible for their own choice of feeling—something that is never honorable.

One's honor is always the admission price for playing the game of control.

******

See Life's Laws
13   Our own life is our sole possession. Just so, it is for everyone.
16   We only control ourselves.
11   **Self-esteem requires integrity.**
26   Change requires the truth of one's heart.

Questions and/or Exercises:
- **When the** issue involves something someone is doing that threatens your physical security, do you think you need to make that person's actions unacceptable?
- **What about** that person?
- **What if** they are doing something that you simply don't like?
- Do you think other people must live their lives to suit you?

The Need to be Accepted

Everyone wants to be accepted. It is a basic human need. Some try to fill that need by trying to change themselves to fit in with others. Some try to change others to be a fit for themselves.

For me, it is about being true to who I am, then looking for others who fit into my life, just being who they are.

Trying to change others, to be who I want, never works. My feelings are the only ones within my control—and accepting only takes me accepting them, and always works. When I stop trying to change them, they feel free to be who they are. Then we both will know if we fit into each other's lives.

It is only when I can accept people for exactly who they are, that I get to know who the other is, and have the people in my life who I want to be there.

✶✶✶✶✶✶

See Life's Laws:
13   Our own life is our sole possession. Just so, it is for everyone.
16   We only control ourselves.
26   Change requires the truth of one's heart.

Questions and/or Exercises:
- **Can you** see, that one of the lies Society has taught us, is that we must have a facade that is acceptable to everyone? Describe your own facade.
- **Do you** think that facade serves or hinders us? *How?*

Acceptance

Accepting someone simply means you don't try—nor even have a need—to change them. Accepting them has nothing to do with liking them.

When someone does not accept you, being exactly who you are, it is not necessarily a bad thing. Could it be, it is just your higher self—yours and theirs—saying stay away, we don't belong together? They're simply saying, "I am someone who won't be happy unless I get to change you."

Still, given this understanding, you can accept them even when they won't accept you. Just heed your higher self and move on in life. Find someone else who accepts and likes you just being you.

******

See Life's Laws:
4   The energy out returns in kind.
17   What we hold with energy runs our lives.
19   We are quintessentially beings of energy.
13   Our own life is our sole possession. Just so, it is for everyone.
16   We only control ourselves.

Questions and/or Exercises:
- **When someone** will only accept you if you change yourself to suit them, can they ever really be a friend?
- **What are** your minimum requirements for being friends? *List them.*
- **Are any** of these things "inherently you"—something only you might require?
- **Is genuinely** caring for one another on your list?

>>><<<

Adoption

People adopt for one of only two reasons: Because they want "that child." Or because they want the child they could not have and are accepting "that child" as a surrogate. A surrogate child will never be good enough, nor will it ever be loved. It is not the "real thing." Is it any wonder that the "higher power"—that God— did not give those particular parents a child?

Will that child love such a parent?—Yes, very likely. That is what innocent children often do. But will that parent know it? If one has not the ability to give it, does one have the ability to know when love is given?

As a surrogate myself, I would ask that if you don't want "that child," only for itself, then please—just get a puppy. A puppy will never grow up to know . . . it is not good enough.

******

See Life's Law:
21   Real love, once given, cannot be taken back.
8   The world is not "out there"—it is "in here."

Questions and/or Exercises:
- **Are you** considering adoption?
- **Are you** clear as to your reasons?
- **Is it because you want "that" child?**
- **If that** is so, then make a list of everything that you like about "that" child.
- **If your** list is short---reconsider

>>><<<

On the Law of Present Living

We are all just painters, painting on the canvas of our lifetime. A painter who has no concept of its size, yet the living always takes place at the point of their brush, in the place called now.

One paints—creates—from the palette of one's past. On it are placed all the colors of the rainbow. Yet some painters choose to mix the colors out of their fears: muddy browns, dark grays, even blacks. They prefer to paint their lives as the storm, and sometimes—though not often—painting the rainbow, like an unattainable mirage.

For the rainbow is comprised of the pure colors of love, the colors of pure joy—the highest essence of the creator. Other painters use those colors in beautiful summer scenes, with sunlight streaming, flowers, clouds, and birds—beauty and joy in every stroke.

What separates the painters and their scenes? They all, are creating on the canvases of their lives, yet the pictures are so different. Some might say that the painters of the storms must somehow want the turmoil of their lives.

Yes, it is true that not all painters' hearts are drawn to the pure colors of the rainbow, to the beauty in the purity of love. But the bottom line truth here is simple: some paint with their fear, while others, with their love.

And what of the canvas? What of the limits of one's lifetime? Is it true that some paint tiny figures, using only little strokes, and in the end the canvas is mostly white, leaving little of themselves to mark this world?

Others paint with wide sweeping strokes of loving abandon, or raging fear—strokes, which in the end fling paint off the canvas; drops of their love, or fear, marking eternity.

******

See Life's Laws:
23 Now is the only time there is.
1   I am the creator.

3   Thoughts are energy: Loving, or not loving (fear).
8   The world is not "out there"—it is "in here."

Questions and/or Exercises:
- **Do you** paint with the colors of your love—or your fear?
- **Is your** painting one of a fearful need to control others—even those you think you love?
- **Hitler, literally** and figuratively, was a painter. He painted the ugliness and stench of the Third Reich. Ironically, some of his earlier painted scenes of beauty were of the places he literally laid to waste in later life. Is that the kind of picture you would paint with your fear?
- **I, too,** have left some shit-stains stinking up my picture. The only way to flush it clean is with the love I paint with now. And so I write these books. What will you do?
- **How will** your picture change between now and when it is finished?
- **Will you** take this book and make it your reprieve?

Feces

There are many things that obstruct our ability to know and to give love. Shame is only one. Shames and "should"—such are as the feces of other people's minds that they would heap upon us. To accept it does not mean we will be fertilized and grow to be better; it just means our viewpoint of life will be obstructed and stink.

******

See Life's Laws:
3   Thoughts are energy.
8   The world is not "out there"—It is "in here."
15   To create a functional life requires one to do one's own thinking.

Questions and/or Exercises:
- **Write down** some of the times you have felt shame.
- **Now note** which were the times that others wiped that shame off onto you, and which were the times you did the wiping all by yourself.
- **Read Law 3**—Is it possible to love someone when immersed in the feces of fear—yours or theirs?

Squeezing Oranges

When life squeezes you, don't expect orange juice. You get to see what's really inside you. Remember, *you are the Creator,* and that's why you arranged to be squeezed. There is something you need to see—in you.

Don't believe you arranged to be squeezed? Look again. You *don't* have the ability to see that one if you *won't* look at what it is in you that you need to see.

That's right. It was YOU who arranged to be squeezed—that highest part of you, your Soul, is in charge of the squeezing. If you refuse the lessons, eventually, it will squeeze even harder until it pops your life like a pimple.

Sad, really . . . when you consider that what comes out of a festering pimple is all you will get out of this life.

******

See Life's Laws:
11   Self-esteem requires integrity.
10   The purpose of life is for those lessons.

Questions and/or Exercises:
- **Do you** agree that everyone occasionally gets squeezed in life?
- **What is** it that comes out of you?
- **Do you** understand that this is the thing your soul demands you look at in order to grow?
- **You don't** believe it? Then consider: Is denying your soul's orders likely to be a healthy thing?

Roots

We all have roots. Like the plants, we too need a root system to channel the energy of acceptance, respect, and love needed to nurture us in life. It is the soil of our family heritage that normally supports us. Their acceptance is like the water that carries the nutrients. Their respect propels it all along. And love? Without love, all life within our souls would simply wither.

The ecosystem of our family plot is needed for our growth and survival. Yet we are not exactly plants. For we have the ability to move about. This ability serves us well when, occasionally, there is no acceptance to be had or little nutrition to be found in the rocky ground of one's judgmental family soil.

Oh, some may choose to whither in life, but those with courage will pull their roots and find more fertile soil, where nutrients flow in the acceptance of others. Perhaps they will no longer have the solace of the family plot, the comforting familiarity of it, but they still have the ability to be nurtured. In fact, they then have the ability to grow far beyond what their family plot ever had to offer.

Should one call this a gift or a curse? Certainly, some will curse them for the very action of moving. "Ungrateful little . . ." Yes, I've heard it too.

And perhaps, it simply doesn't matter—not to one who just accepts "what is." Perhaps one then becomes the nurturing soil those orphaned others need. Perhaps one then starts a new family plot. Perhaps one then leaves a new family legacy. Perhaps then, the whole world is nurtured. Perhaps. . . .

******

See Life's Laws:
5   For every sorrowful thing, there exists the potential for equal joy. The Universe always balances.
19 We are quintessentially beings of energy.
12 Our lives are run first by our needs, then our wants.
18 Soul-to-soul pacts are made in the pre-existence.

Questions and/or Exercises:
- **How well** does your family plot support you in life? *Explain.*
- **If it doesn't**, have you moved on?
- **If it doesn't**, and you haven't, will you?

Social Creatures

We are social creatures. We all need each other. It is the connection itself we need so much to feel. Social creatures don't do life well alone. Yet aren't we all—on that higher, spiritual level of our minds and hearts—connected? When one gets past the pain, that energy of fear, with which we cloud our minds—gets to know the energy of one's love fully—*then* is when one sees that higher spiritual connection, and really feels it. *Then,* is when we need no one, yet connect with everyone.

******

See Life's Laws:
3   Thoughts are energy: Loving, or not loving (fear).
17   What we hold with energy runs our lives.
19   We are quintessentially beings of energy.

Questions and/or Exercises:
- **How social** a creature are you?
- **Do you** play the "Lone Ranger," crying inside for that connection, but afraid to reach out for it with love? Write about any long, cold, lonely ride you've taken in your past.
- **Do you know** that if you don't have love for yourself, you have none to offer others?

No Secrets

There are no secrets, just things we refuse to see consciously. In my higher mind, I know everything about you—and you, me. On that level, there are no secrets. And on that level, we are so much more than we can ever consciously conceive.

******

See Life's Laws:
19   We are quintessentially beings of energy.
20   We are part of the energy that comprises God.

Questions and/or Exercises:
- **What if** who we are on that level is simply love?
- **And were** that true, do you think being conscious of—that believing it as fact—might cause us to treat one another better?
- **Will you** consider believing it?

The Two-sided Mirror

There have been known cases in which someone, blind from birth, has been given the ability to see. They literally had to learn what they were seeing by the use of the previous experience of it–touch, smell, hearing. An apple was not recognized until the eyes were closed, and it was held, smelled, and then tasted. Just so, I experience you, only through the existing experience of me—kind of like looking in a mirror.

There is a Spiritual Law which states: You are but a mirror in which I can see me. Basically, it says that what I see in you that I don't like, is but a reflection of what I don't like in me. Kind of like looking at each other through a two-sided mirror; we each see only aspects of ourselves.

Isn't it scary that the person we each see when regarding one another is always a perfectly shielded reflection of ourselves? Isn't it amazing that we communicate at all? Do you see how, when looking at our reflection, there is always a choice: To war with everything unlovable in ourselves, or to love everything in our own perfect grace? It's all there to see—and it's all about me when looking through a two-sided mirror at you.

The real question is: to see through that two-sided mirror, am I willing to see the true beauty of you, knowing I must use eyes I have never used? Will I look inward, close my eyes, smell, taste, and savor? Will I own the exquisite essence of my aroma, taste the delicious flavors of me? Will I choose to experience and be nourished by the truth of all this beauty within me? And then—only then—reach out with that energy to experience you, and what you have to add to me. The energy of pure love is required to see through a two-sided mirror. Were it to be given a name, I believe that two-sided mirror could be called "Namaste."

Note:
'Namaste' is a cultural and religious word from the Hindu religion that roughly translates to: *"My Divine soul recognizes the Divine soul in you."*

*****

See Life's Laws:
3   Thoughts are energy: Loving, or not loving (fear).
7   Blame is the abdication of responsibility.
9   Others are but a mirror for us to see ourselves.
8   The world is not "out there"—it is "in here."
19   We are quintessentially beings of energy.
15   One must do one's own thinking.

Questions and/or Exercises:
- **Do you** find it easier to look for and see the darkness, the negative, the fearful part of yourself?
- **Do you** realize that this is as it is, for nearly everyone?
- **Wouldn't it** be so much better to look for and find the love?
- **If you did**, how would your life be different?

>>><<<

A Gifted Few

It's all about the lessons . . .

Mostly, we ignore them. Some take them to the grave, unacknowledged, unlearned—and un-lived. Sometimes it takes the final whispers from Death himself to speak of them in a way we will hear. Only a courageous few then receive the gift of Death's lessons and survive long enough to live them.

******

See Life's Laws:
10   The purpose of life is for those lessons.
18   Soul-to-soul pacts are made in the pre-existence.

Questions and/or Exercises:
- **Do you** think that Death's lessons are the gift this book is offering you? This is what I intend it to be—a gift.
- **Do you** understand that within this gift—this reprieve—this book, there are no expectations being held by me that you accept it? Some will—some won't; what is your choice and why?
- **This gift** was given to me, and not offering it to you would be unthinkable.
- **If it helps** make your life better, will you do any less than offer it to someone you love?

About Respect and Disrespect

Respect is something I think and feel—and yes, do—toward someone. Respect uplifts us both. It is uplifting in spirit, as well as in standing in the community.

Disrespect now is not such a mutual thing. Yes, I think it and feel it. And most of all, disrespect is something I do. Thing is—given someone who has self-respect, it doesn't necessarily bring down that person's energy. Nor does it lower that person's standing in the community.

But it will always have those effects upon me.

******

See Life's Law:
19   We are quintessentially beings of energy.

Questions and/or Exercises:
- **On that** soul level, we are all spirits of equal magnificence. Don't you think that requires a certain respect, no matter who they are, here and now?
- **Sometimes that** is a hard feat to do, honestly. If you are unwilling to do it, will you at least respect your soul by not disrespecting them?

>>><<<

The Currency of Esteem

Respect is the currency of a person's esteem. A generous person gives it freely and abundantly upon first meeting another. Then, depending upon that new person's integrity, more might be given, or all might be lost.

But sometimes, as in one Vet to another, there is a debt that is beyond the currency of simple respect. Can it be any other way, when a person has been willing to put their life on the line with yours?

******

See Life's Laws:
11   Self-esteem requires integrity.
13   Our own life is our sole possession. Just so, it is for everyone.
19   We are quintessentially beings of energy.

Questions and/or Exercises:
➤ **If you** are not a Vet, can you understand?
➤ **If you** are, do you need an explanation?

Vet to Vet

Some fought—Some died . . .

Hell, just being a vet

says you put your life

on the line . . .

with mine.

What our differences now

may not reflect,

is the fact that you,

just being a vet,

will always command

this vet's respect!

Support

Some say that having my own cheering section is necessary to a joyful life. It's true—but only when I am among the supporting members.

******

See Life's Laws:
19   We are quintessentially beings of energy.
6   The energy of thoughts must flow.

Questions and/or Exercises:
- **Does your** world revolve for you, or with you?
- **Do you** give as much as you take?
- **Do you** find joy in serving others? *Again, discuss.*

Waiting on a Friend

All we really get coming into this life is a little time. It could be said that time is life.

So when someone repeatedly makes appointments with me, then asks me to wait . . .

What they are saying to me is: ". . . my time is more important than yours: my life, worth more than yours."

To wait patiently for them to get ready is to allow myself to fall victim. Likely, it is not a conscious thing in their mind. And it is to definitely validate this viewpoint they are expressing about me, into my own mind. Is giving my time—my life—away to a friend really such an admirable thing? In accepting the situation, are we either one, being a friend?

Truth is, if you don't respect my time, you don't respect me—and in time, by allowing it, neither will I.

******

See Life's Laws:
13   Our own life is our sole possession. Just so, it is for everyone.
10   The purpose of life is for those lessons.
18   Soul-to-soul pacts are made in the pre-existence.

Questions and/or Exercises:
- Do you often make your friends wait?
- **If so,** and they refused to wait, would you still consider them your friend?
- **Is it possible** that it is you, not being a friend? ***Discuss it with them.***

Validations

Whenever the shit's in your face, it's either a lesson, a test, or a validation. Lessons and tests are usually given by a teacher. Does this mean that validations are to tell you that you got the lessons, have passed the tests, and are now teachers?

Not really! Truth is, you—that is, your soul—was always your teacher. Others and events are just the lessons your soul prepared. Yes, when not learned and passed, the lessons and tests just get harder. But when passed—

The validations? —The validations get absolutely orgasmic!

******

See Life's Laws:
18   Soul-to-soul pacts are made in the pre-existence.
10   The purpose of life is for those lessons.

Questions and/or Exercises:
- **Everyone has** some recurring shit that keeps splattering them in the face. What's yours?
- **What do you** think the lesson behind it could be?
- **If you find** it easy to answer this last question, that is *not* it. Whatever the true lesson, it is one you do *not* want to look at. ***Question is, will you?***

The Sting of Truth

People will always talk. But when we get angry with what they say about us, perhaps it would be wise to remember, the angrier we are, the more their words have carried the sting of truth.

See Life's Law:
9   Others are but a mirror for us to see ourselves.

Questions and/or Exercises:
- **Has someone said** something about you recently that really pissed you off? *Write it down.*
- **Now, what** part of it do you know is true?
- **Is there** a part that you don't believe is true?
- **Are you** willing to look with honesty? The part you know to be true is not the part that pisses you off—take a look at the other part. There is something there you don't want to see.

>>><<<

Pretense

Change? —Change most often comes on the heels of discomfort or necessity, but only when the change is about you. As for changing others, the game of control is just too strong. It has always gotten you what you wanted from others—*or so you believe.* But you don't see that the game is really one of pretense. Any change you may demand and get from others is merely a pretense.

Real change is always personal—something no one can do to or for you. Change is something one cannot do, except for oneself.

※※※※※※

See Life's Laws:
16   We only control ourselves.
13   Our own life is our sole possession. Just so, it is for everyone.
26   **Change requires** the truth of one's heart.
8   **The world** is not "out there"—it is "in here."
24   **What we** dwell upon with energy is what we attract.

Questions and/or Exercises:
- **Are you** aware that changing your mind can be an instantaneous thing?
- **Do you** know that the resulting change in your life can also be instantaneous?
- **Don't think** so? You're right!—But only because your world will always come to you the way you see it. *Y'know?*

>>><<<

Expensive People

Expensive people like to take offense. It's not that I ever intended to GIVE offense. Fact is—it is not that I did.

Offense is not something one can *"give,"* rather something one must *"take."* With the taking, one demands payment in the currency of your energy. Ah, the expense of having people like that in your life. . . .

Maybe expensive people are simply not worth having around. They just take your energy—while giving nothing back. With expensive people, it is not who you are, but who they want you to be. And more often than not, the "who" you are is only a figment of their own imagination.

It's not that I'm stingy or poor. What they have is just not something I'm buying. I'm choosy about how I spend my energy in this life.

******

See Life's Laws:
8   The world is not "out there"—it is "in here."
19   We are quintessentially beings of energy.
13   Our own life is our sole possession. Just so, it is for everyone.

Questions and/or Exercises:
- **Do you** need to be more choosy about how and with whom you spend your life?
- **Who in** your life is expensive?
- **Being as** this is your one and only life, does anyone have the right to make demands on how you spend it?
- **Do you** ever make such demands upon others? Are you an expensive person?

No Fear

A man is not brave who has no fear—just foolish.

A man who is brave steps through his fear when he knows he must.

A wise man is one who knows when he must.

A truly functional man knows his fear is really only about change—the unknown. And, does this change merely concern the way he lives his life? Or is it about no longer living life?—because *that* is the one kind of fear that may demand physical steps. The others only demand acceptance.

******

See Life's Laws:
3   Thoughts are energy: Loving, or not loving (fear).
17   What we hold with energy runs our lives.
14   Change is the constant of the Universe.

Questions and/or Exercises:
- **Are you** one of the "foolish" brave people? Or, what is it you fear just now?
- **Is the** fear about some physical danger? Or about a change to your life and your feelings about it?
- **What steps** do you need take to get through it? *And will you take them?*

You Are The Teacher

That higher part of your mind connected to God, creates everything you consciously, but mostly unconsciously, accept you are worthy of having.

That "mostly unconscious" part of your mind is taught by the lessons of what you think, say, and do in every experience you have. That *"do"* part is the truth of your thinking *expressed.* It is so often expressed unconsciously, like a reflex—*because you seldom pay conscious attention to your thinking.*

Make no mistake; The Law states that *Thoughts Create.* It is you who are the teacher of your unconscious mind—and those unconscious reflex experiences show the truth of your thinking. Of those things you *"do"* so unconsciously?—Make a conscious effort to know the truth of the *"why,"* you do them, for those are the truths that keep you from having everything you want.

******

See Life's Laws:
1   I am the creator.
22   We consciously only feel our own feelings.
20   We are part of the energy that comprises God.

Questions and/or Exercises:
   ➢ **What did** you think, say, and do so unconsciously today? Make a list.
   ➢ **Ask yourself** how well those things align with what you want—of the *"who"* you see yourself as being.
   ➢ **Unconsciously or** consciously, you do create what you want. Those things you don't think match your conscious wants, what is the truth? Because you do unconsciously want them?

Forgiveness—The Stupid Shit

People will always say and do those stupid-shit things that you think are wrong. Then you find yourself having to go through the process of *"forgiving."* Thing is, would you ever need to forgive them if *you* hadn't judged *them* as *wrong* in the first place?

Truth is, forgiveness is about changing your perception of *them*, and about *forgiving yourself* for having been so *judgmental* and *unloving*.

This might be well remembered for the next time you start to judge another person. Then, if you think you are forgiving *them*, you will know that *you are still in the grip of being judgmental.*

But hey! You will forever be caught in the cycle of judging people wrong, then having to forgive them. That is, unless?—

Unless you can realize that right and wrong don't exist, except in someone's judgmental mind! And why would anyone want to have a judgmental mind? Why do *you* want to see someone as somehow *"wrong"*—unless it is your way of seeing yourself as *right*, and them, somehow *not as good as?* Do you think—hmmmm?

Ah, but let's cut through our own *stupid-shit* stuff. Let's look at it in the framework of those Spiritual Laws. You see, beyond all that, is the simple fact that they are merely offering you the chance to learn something—some lesson that your own soul feels you need to learn.

Yes, you and I just went through the process of peeling this particular onion. Can you see how going directly to the Spiritual Laws can cut through and avoid a lot of that "stupid-shit stuff" in your life?

******

See Life's Laws:
7   Blame is the abdication of responsibility.
9   Others are but a mirror for us to see ourselves.
18 Soul-to-soul pacts are made in the pre-existence.
10 The purpose of life is for those lessons.

Questions and/or Exercises:
- **Can you** see that *right and wrong—good and bad* are a dysfunctional way of judging others? Why?
- **Could** *loving or unloving* be a more functional way? Why?
- **Which way** did your religion teach you to judge?
- **Did your** religion also teach that it is the other person who needs your forgiveness? What do you think now?

Then there is Forgiveness—The Serious Shit

Yes, and then there are those things that people sometimes do that actually cause real harm to you or a loved one—things that are way beyond the *"dumb shit"* stuff that you simply don't like. These are the things that are extremely painful, physically or mentally. Sure, the mental stuff is pain we take on ourselves, but often it is pain that is unavoidable, given we are all human.

Again, we are talking way beyond the stupid shit stuff we dislike—way beyond that into feelings of hatefulness and revenge. Now those kinds of feelings are as chains, connecting us to that other person forever and draining our reserve of energy.

Like a vampire sucking upon your very soul, it will run your life until you break the chain. Then, is when it may help to see that other person as being *"less than"* they could be. As such, they are not worth the energy you are expending, it is so much easier to break that chain.

We are given the choice by the Creator to live in the energy of love or that energy that is not love, rather fear. That other person is someone who lives in that fearful place where there is no love. It is through your pity that the chain can be broken. Their soul is just as magnificent as your own, but what they are doing to it is undeniably something to be pitied.

Empathy is when you connect with another person through love. Pity is different; it is to disconnect yourself. We are all beings of energy, remember. To stay connected through love would still be draining to your soul. You don't *empathize,* you don't *forgive,* you *pity!*

The fact is, there are people in this world you *don't* want to be connected with energetically. Yes, it is a hard lesson to learn that sometimes to love yourself requires you to consciously disconnect from someone else.

Once you have healed and are no longer holding any energy on it, *then* you will find that the Universe is in balance because you will accept that they are who they are, and that you have stopped wanting to change them, and you may have even found something about the situation, for which you are thankful.

Ah, but given that this process is one way of getting through the pain, *I don't recommend it!* I have to admit, it is the "stupid shit" exercise in onion, the onion-peeling way of going about—or around—it. Taking this one directly to the Laws is for the truly courageous. Not everyone is ready or willing to learn this lesson in courage.

Here is the hard truth. Life is about the lessons. If this was about something they did that harmed you physically, then let's hope you learned to avoid that in the future.

If it was something that caused you pain mentally, then take responsibility. *You are the creator of your life—you create every bit of the mental pain that is in it.* And remember: you are the one who has to feel it—they do not.

They did what they did. "Did"—past tense. You cannot change it, and you have not accepted it. When you refuse to accept what you cannot change, you guarantee yourself pain. Seeing them as someone not worth it and disconnecting your energy is one way to ease the pain. Seeing them as someone to be pitied—is two. But to hit the jackpot requires you to stop banging your head into that solid brick wall of unacceptance—the one you won't admit is there. *It is what it is.* If you don't want it running the rest of your life, then accept it and move on. Only then will you be open to finding the gift in the experience—there is one, you know?

******

See Life's Laws:
5   For every sorrowful thing, there exists the potential for equal joy. The Universe always balances.
17 What we hold with energy runs our lives.
19 We are quintessentially beings of energy.

Questions and/or Exercises:
- **Is there** someone in your life who has harmed you to such an extent? One who, like a vampire, still sucks your energy?
- **Can you** see that it is not about them sucking, but rather you spewing it at them?
- **Do you** have the courage to stop—to break the connection—and just accept?
- **Do you** have the wisdom to then look for the gift? *Again, there is one y'know?*
- **Or are** you choosing instead to be pissed at me for telling you this?

Little Flying Lizards

Often, others label you as a coward when they see your fear. The truth is, you are not, until you, yourself, put on that label. Every human on the planet has fears. A fear is only an imaginary dragon in your mind. It generally starts as a little flying lizard sent by your higher self out of love, to caution and warn you of perceived danger. Then it is blown up large, fed by your conscious mind using the winds of possibility. We believe ourselves cowards—those of us who won't walk the dragon, until it is once again, a little lizard.

✶✶✶✶✶✶

See Life's Law:
8   The world is not "out there"—it is "in here." *Only you can change your mind.*

Questions and/or Exercises:
- **Again, is** this dragon withering and dying for lack of being fed?
- **Or is it** growing stronger, gorging on the mental shit coming out the ass-end of your mind?

>>><<<

Tigers

Your fears are generally unfounded—only the imaginary dragons of your mind. Yet strongly emotional unpleasant feelings are *always* tigers, and *never* imaginary. Yes, your feelings are real and can, and often will, devour you. What is not real is that they are created by someone somewhere outside of your mind, and that they have to be tigers. *Only when you own them can they then become pussy cats.*

******

See Life's Laws:
7   **Blame is** the abdication of responsibility.
8   **The world** is not "out there"—it is "in here."
17   **What we** hold with energy runs our lives.

Questions and/or Exercises:
- **It is much** better to pet that before it becomes a tiger. Staving off someone else's tiger with a chair is generally a losing proposition. Question is: When it concerns another person's feelings, who needs to do the petting? Hint: It is *not* you.
- **Flip side:** If they are your own feelings—NOW who needs to do the petting?
- **Guy, or girl**, if you are in a relationship and busy blaming your partner for your choice of bad feelings—well, that just makes you the fearful little pussy who refuses to own that responsibility. My question to you—*ownerless pussy*—is: How long do you think it will be before your raging tiger consumes the relationship?

Feeding Frenzy

Feeding sharks or hearts; what's the difference? —They both are hungry. Sometimes, both go into a feeding frenzy. Perhaps it's only that a loving heart won't take your arm off—not while living in the space of love.

Although there are those who might feel the shark is the better deal, given that some hearts live in the energy of *fear* rather than *love*. And clearly, that would be a heart to which one knows better than to get too close. *A heart that vacillates between love and fear is the one most likely to bite, and it will be in your behind.*

******

See Life's Laws:
3   Thoughts are energy: Loving, or not loving (fear).
8   The world is not "out there"—it is "in here."
17   What we hold with energy runs our lives.

Questions and/or Exercises:
- **Do you** think you can ever be close in your relationship if yours is a heart that vacillates?
- **Ladies, do** you feel your man is just chumming your shark, feeding you what they think you want to hear? You might want to rein in that shark?—and address your man only with your love, never your fear. *What do you think?*
- **And guys,** it's not just the ladies getting lied to by the men, but the reason both might lie is likely the same. Could it be that both are afraid of getting bit by the other's shark—that the cost of telling the truth will be a chunk out of your ass?
- **The only** thing that *feeds* a relationship is love. Why would you ever vacillate it into fear—don't you know, fear *feeds on* your relationship? *Write down your thoughts about it.*

One's Way of Life

Sometimes, with the death of one's old way of life, there remains a restless spirit—a spirit unable to sleep until it can say goodbye to all it has loved who are no longer part of the new. Such spirits reside in each of us, and to have rest in the new life, one must bring them to a loving completion.

Such a completion is called acceptance. It is you, accepting that person you loved, being exactly who they are. And you recognizing that it was you, making them wrong, and you, now forgiving yourself. *Your forgiveness is never about anyone but yourself.*

✶✶✶✶✶✶

See Life's Law:
17   What we hold with energy runs our lives.

Questions and/or Exercises:
- **It was** with purpose that I did not put this reflection in close proximity to the ones on forgiveness. Why do you think that is?
- **In repeating** the same concept, but in a different way, it's true that one may hear and accept only one. Of those who understood it all, does repeating it dilute its meaning? Or is this thought more about the death of one's old way of life, and not so much about forgiveness?
- **What if** reading this book would cause the death of your current way of life? Would you continue reading it? *Change your mind, change your life*—Y'know?

About Song

A song is the voice's connection to the soul, to all that personal "God the Creator" power. Even ancient man knew this; perhaps modern man has just forgotten—it seems he now uses it for frivolous things. Just look at the lyrics of some popular songs . . .

How many are uplifting to the soul? With those that are, then is when we can feel our soul take flight. But with those that aren't . . . remember that guy's "pretty little four wheel drive?" That one caters only to those who are mean-spirited!

✱✱✱✱✱✱

See Life's Laws:
19   We are quintessentially beings of energy.
3   Thoughts are energy: Loving, or not loving (fear).

Questions and/or Exercises:
- **The tune** may be catchy, but do the words—the sentiments—uplift your soul? *List some that do for you.*
- **Songs expressing** sentiments of revenge—can you see that they only validate someone who sees themselves as a victim? Do such songs validate you?
- **Me? I'm just** a redneck, remember? And I dearly love my ". . . pretty little souped-up four wheel drive."—*Know that song?* **Write about the sentiments it suggests. Do they uplift you?**

Courage

Again, courage is not about facing death; it is about living life while facing fear. Courage is always preceded by the fear, normally of things that haven't yet happened. It might be wise to remember that with the energy of that fear itself, we are busy creating, or attracting into our lives, the very thing we fear—right now.

******

See Life's Laws:
2 Thoughts create.
3 Thoughts are energy: Loving, or not loving (fear).
24 What we dwell upon with energy is what we attract.

Questions and/or Exercises:
- ➢ Do you remember the Law: ***Whatever our thoughts dwell upon with energy is what we are attracting into our life right now?*** What are the things you most fear right now?
- ➢ **Do you** really want to create your life to be precisely what you ***don't*** want?
- ➢ **Do you** now see how important it is to face life with courage? ***Write about it.***

Earning Respect

Do you think that with those folks who demand you earn their respect, it is because they feel that giving respect somehow takes something away from them—something they're too socially and emotionally cheap to give? Maybe so—

But could the real truth be that it is only about getting control? If you jump through their hoops long enough, they may decide they like you. But respect you? —Not a chance. Such people are not givers of respect; they're takers of your energy.

******

See Life's Laws:
19   We are quintessentially beings of energy.
7   Blame is the abdication of responsibility.

Questions and/or Exercises:
- **Are there** people in your life whose respect you want, but don't feel you get? *List them.*
- **Have you** ever felt depleted just by being around them? *Write about it.*
- **Do you** not see that control is a fallacy, but that the energy they suck from you in the effort to control is not? *Note down your thoughts on all of it.*

Needs and Wants

There are physical needs that sometimes require the help of others to sustain your body. But the mental—those also often require the help of someone else, but only to make you aware of those needs. But the meeting with them always requires only you. No one who knows themselves is ever needy. Because knowing yourself is the only true mental need, there is.

And wants? Only when your needs are met can you deal with wants. Until then, the needs, consciously or unconsciously, run your life.

The Universe/God gives us everything we need. With the mental needs, help usually comes in the form of a "significant other," who will stir up your life and help you get to know yourself—mirrors, remember?

Once you've done your part, your relationships will never again be needy. They then become about someone you simply want to be with, someone you will accept exactly as they are. And maybe—just maybe—in light of your example, they will do the same.

✶✶✶✶✶✶

See Life's Laws:
9   Others are but a mirror for us to see ourselves.
8   The world is not "out there"—it is "in here."
12 Our lives are run first by our needs, then our wants.
18 Soul-to-soul pacts are made in the pre-existence.

Questions and/or Exercises:
- **Of the** needs we are talking about here? Those physical ones are about sustaining your life. The mental—those are the true needs of your soul. *Write about it.*
- **Why do** you think that is?
- **Could it be** that it is the experience of it—of knowing yourself in this physical life—that, is what your soul craves?
- **Would that** then mean that the reason you are here in life is to gain the experience your soul needs to grow and evolve? *Keep writing—keep breathing.*

My Viewpoint In Redneck Speak

You know how a new swimmer tries to throw their head back, to keep their mouth and nose above the water at all times? Eventually, most will give that up and just accept that sometimes it's necessary to just close their mouth to the reality of it occasionally being under the surface. Now that is functional. And then sometimes, there are those who just won't.

They are the ones who go through life with their head kinked back to hold their mouth and nose up out of the realities of being human. Are they afraid someone might've pissed in the pool?

Could it be that they *know* someone has—from personal experience?

Even so, with their mouth held above the pissy waters of humanity, it is always free to tell others what they "should" do—and also to take offense when they don't. While it is nice to never need to shut one's mouth or to keep opinions to oneself, it does create one big personal problem. It's hard to maintain that posture when it puts such a strain on the neck.

So, to make it easier on themselves, they use a stick as a prop to hold their heads up in that superior position. And the only way to do that is to insert that stick up their butt.

Then there's the problem that they just can't see. What with their viewpoint always looking at something loftier than everyone else's—kinda makes it hard for them to see that no one likes or appreciates them. It's only when they find someone whom they themselves like that their stick then becomes just a little too uncomfortable. Rather than take responsibility, it's just easier to blame and to take offense at things that were never meant to be offensive. Yes, it is a heartbreaking thing when one keeps running those whom they've come to care about, right out of their lives, and can't see why.

But hey, their field of view doesn't allow them to see. About the only thing that will is when someone comes along who cares enough to give that stick a good tug. A stick like that likely has become such a part of their person that they've forgotten it being there. But a stick like that is a dangerous thing. What if someone were just to jerk it out? After the ensuing explosion, that stick will just be put back in its uncomfortable, but familiar place—such a dysfunctional crutch.

The fact is, no one has the right to remove another's stick. And it is such a rare—even stellar—occurrence, when a person has the courage to deal with the humiliating experience of pulling their stick out and exposing what has really been inside—how that stick has been keeping their shit from stinking for so long. The only way it can even be done is by rejecting the reason it was installed in the first place—that is, by being themselves, and not giving a shit about what other people think.

Bottom line: Isn't that what that whole "nose-in-the-air" facade was all about in the first place—them wanting others to think they were "better than?" It seems to me that they could do with a little "essence of redneck."

Yeah, hey—I'm just a redneck. One who "don't-give-a-shit-what-you-think" simply because he doesn't need to be better than you, to like who he is. No—this redneck *"don't . . . neeed . . . no . . . steeen-king . . . steee-ck,"* just to like himself.

See Life's Laws:
8   The world is not "out there"—it is "in here."
17   What we hold with energy runs our life.
7   Blame is the abdication of responsibility.

Questions and/or Exercises:
- **Can you** see that the whole thing is summed up by that one phrase: by. . . "don't-give-a-shit-what-you-think." Do you think that's a negative thing?
- **What if** "negative and positive" were also just an expression of your personal judgments—like "right and wrong?"
- **Is running** your life in fear of what other people will think, a positive thing? What do you think?
- **And that** stick mentioned?—Could be it's just a simile for "better than?"
- **If you've** got one, I suspect you now know it. I just gave it a loving little tug. *Y'know?*

About Offensive People

There are mean-spirited acts, and there are acts of goodwill. Both are of equal service in determining with whom I want to associate.

So, when by their actions, someone is showing me the meanness of their spirit—and assuming there is no personal threat—why would I want to take offense? Aren't they doing me a service?

******

See Life's Laws:
8   The world is not "out there"—it is "in here."
19   We are quintessentially beings of energy.
3   Thoughts are energy: Loving, or not loving (fear).

Questions and/or Exercises:
- **Do you** agree that "perception is a choice?"
- **Do you** see that your feelings are also a choice?
- **In the** choice of your perception, and/or your feelings, what changes could you make that would better serve you in life?

Book Two
PART THREE

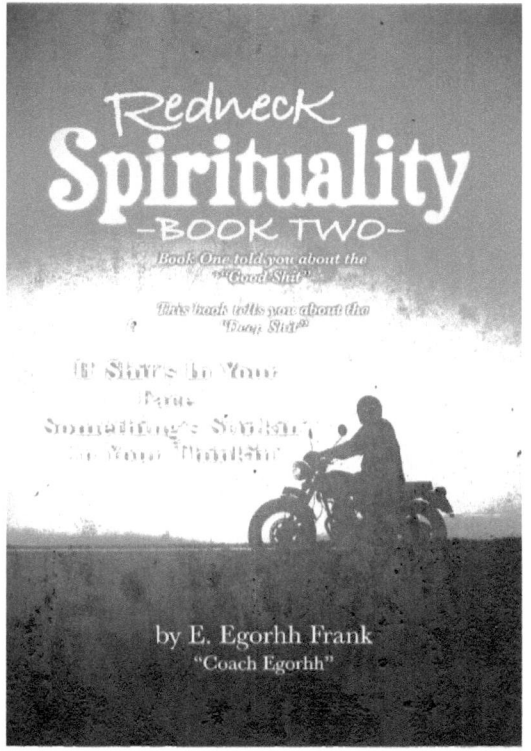

Reflections of Love
In the Light of the Laws

Unconditional Love

In a relationship where there is unconditional love, there is also ultimate freedom. That is what loving unconditionally means. Each has the inalienable right to be exactly who they are and still be loved and accepted. No one ever pays a price for honesty.

Got dishonesty in your relationship? —Maybe you need to look for where your love may be conditional.

See Life's Laws:
21   Real love, once given, cannot be taken back.
13   Our own life is our sole possession. Just so, it is for everyone.

Questions and/or Exercises:
- **Do you** get that real love is always unconditional/ What conditions have you placed on your own love? *Write about it.*
- **If yours** is unconditional, but theirs isn't, are you willing to be their teacher?
- **Can you** accept that they may not learn? If you can't—then you gotta know: ***Your love is still conditional.***

Accepting

I hear people complaining about their significant others and often want to tell them the hard truth that they don't want to hear. It is only with the rare one who asks that I speak. Most people have to be drowning before they will reach out for what they need. Some even prefer to drown, rather than face the truth about themselves.

And the truth about you and me? The simple truth is, we don't have the right to jump into anyone's life without being invited. And even then, neither of us is so above the other that we can save them.

The fact that you are reading this book, I consider to be your invitation for me to speak. Still, this book is a waste of your time if you don't want something better in life. *And I would have to accept that about you.* If I didn't, it would not be because you aren't acceptable. Again, it would be about me not accepting you.

So now, I started out talking about relationships . . .

If you are unhappy with your significant other, then the relationship is a waste of time for you both—*that is, if . . .* you don't want to change *"you"* to make it better. If you do, then consider it is not because she (or he) is not acceptable, being exactly who they are. Yes, you've got it; it is because *you* aren't accepting of *them.*

Your life is not about anyone but you. That they are in your life is only because they were sent by a higher power to point out every unlovable thing there is about you. It's about those things that could make you a better person; were you to just look at, and truly own them—and sometimes . . . change.

Are they really unlovable—or are you just unloving?

******

See Life's Laws:
9 Others are but a mirror for us to see ourselves.
8 The world is not "out there"—it is "in here."
18 Soul-to-soul pacts are made in the pre-existence.
10 The purpose of life is for those lessons.
13 Our own life is our sole possession. Just so, it is for everyone.

Questions and/or Exercises:
- **There are** four basic messages here. *List what you think they are. If you think you may have missed something, come back after you have finished this book and do this one again.*
- **Is there** anything about these simple messages you cannot accept? If so, turn back to Part Two and read Law 7. *Then write about what you then see. These questions and exercises are deliberately vague because the understandings here are critical to having a successful relationship. I can't save you, nor can this book. But it can be a **flotation device for you to save yourself.***

About Relationships

What does it take to make a good relationship between a person and their mate? I'd have to say safety and honesty.

That is safety, both physically and emotionally. Each must know the other would never harm them physically or reject them emotionally—no matter what.

And honesty?—Honesty is a much stickier matter. Knowing we have that emotional safety—that you will never be made to pay an emotional price for your honesty with me, requires we both be willing to search within, for the truth about our feelings. Why am I feeling angry/sad/upset about what you have said or done? I must understand and deal with my own feelings—*but mainly, I must own them.* Only when I can deal with you without blame, can we—either one—truly have anything that approaches honesty.

I know, it sounds pretty esoteric. In the *"real world,"* it is just so much easier to make them pay for *your choice* of feelings—Yeah, in that world, *they're going to pay!* But then, so will you. You surely don't expect them to be honest with you when the only way they can avoid your revenge is to tell you the lie you want to hear.

******

See Life's Laws:
7   Blame is the abdication of responsibility.
8   The world is not "out there"—it is "in here."

Questions and/or Exercises:
- **Have you** ever had a significant other lie to you?
- **Do you** now understand why? *Explain.*

Odd Thoughts

Something I've learned about relationships:

Growing or dying, life never stops and takes a breath. It's always changing, always heading somewhere. If you both don't have the same place in mind somewhere down the road —you just don't get there together.

******

See Life's Laws:
14   Change is the constant of the Universe.
8   The world is not "out there"—it is "in here."
13   Our own life is our sole possession. Just so, it is for everyone.

Questions and/or Exercises:
- ➤ **Have you** discussed with your significant other exactly where it is you want to go in life?
- ➤ **Is it the** same place? *Write about it.*
- ➤ **If you haven't**, *don't you think you might want to give them a heads-up on this one?*

>>><<<

The Truth About Commitment

Relationships are a constant balancing act—balancing what one receives from the relationship with what one gives. The moment one side of the scale slams full-up, it's inevitable that someone will fall off. Sustaining the balance is always a two-party effort. For the balance is a touchy thing. Is what you are giving something they want to receive? Maybe it is you who won't accept—receive—what they are giving? And maybe one is just too stingy with their love?— We are talking about love here—giving and receiving it in the way we want it—y'know. In the end, it only takes one to part. And it matters not if that one simply gets off or falls off.

And parting?—It is not always a physical thing. Some will claim commitment and choose to stay together. They are the liars in life. This is your own life, and it cannot be given away to another, not without being dishonest to your soul. *Commitment can only be to one's self in one's own life, to being the best person one can be. Commitment to someone else is always a lie! If you are there in support of them, it is only because you want to be.*

It is a lie you tell first to your own soul, and then to other's. It is told because it supports your greatest fear—the fear that you aren't lovable. The fear that you—or they—won't be able to hold, or be worthy of the other's love.

Staying with someone you no longer love is an even more insidious lie. Real love, once given, can never be taken back. If you no longer love them, then the truth is, *you never loved them at all.* Real love or not, relationships require balance.

Relationships are always about meeting one another's needs. Only the really great ones involve real love. The others?—The others are simply based on fear. One can recognize them by the demands for commitment—the promises in those lies—and then all the drama and the struggle for control that inevitably follows.

The needs are about balancing the love remember, not about balancing your fears. Bottom line: relationships provide the perfect place and the perfect person to give you the lessons in life you need to grow past your fears and learn to love. The trick is that when you fall off that horse, get back on. You may be in for a few rough rides, and it could take a whole herd of horses, but eventually, you will learn to love.

******

See Life's Laws:
21 Real love, once given, cannot be taken back.
13 Our own life is our sole possession. Just so, it is for everyone.
12 Our lives are run by our needs, then our wants.
10 The purpose of life is for those lessons.

Questions and/or Exercises:
- **Do you stay** because you want to, or because of some lie called commitment?
- **Have you the** courage to love without assurance—the "courage" part requires you to chance they may not feel the same way—y'know?
- **If your** relationship's over, and there are hard feelings, be sure they are not yours. Only then can your next one be someone you love—indeed, have you learned how to love? *Write about that one.*

About Proving One's Love

If you want your mate to prove their love—or to fight for your own—you are not a person going about the business of *love;* rather, you are going about the business of *control.* You are not a person *"in love."* You are a person *"in fear."* Perhaps most of all, your fear is that someday your mate will see this truth.

And truth? —Truth is, they will never win your love. Nor will you win control. Both are things that have to be given.

It might be wise to consider that control can be taken back, but real love, once given, is never taken back. Real love cannot be given or accepted by someone who is just concerned with a fearful need to control. *Love and fear are the only two energies we live by, and they can never mix—remember?*

******

See Life's Laws:
- 3   Thoughts are energy: Loving, or not loving (fear).
- 16   We only control ourselves.
- 21   Real love, once given, cannot be taken back.

Questions and/or Exercises:
- **Do you** see that with love, there is no *fighting*, there is no *winning*—there is only *accepting*?
- **Do you** have the courage not to fear love?—You do know that there cannot be love, if there is fear—don't you? If you have a grasp on these Laws of Life, then this answer will be clear. *If not, re-read the above laws—the long form—in Part Two. Then write about it*

Magnets

Everyone has a personal magnet. Most insist on marking the opposite ends as *right and wrong*. Yet such labels do, in fact, have no real meaning, as they are never exactly the same in anyone else's mind. Why not label with what is truth in every heart?—Things that sustain one's soul and things that don't.

Yes, the poles are clear when marked only *love* and *fear*. Being human, I am the magnet: a curious mixture of both. Being aware, I know from which end I want to attract. Do the chameleons called *"right" and "wrong,"* really give one that possibility? The truth is that, however mislabeled, our magnets are the same. It's just that being "right," keeps some from being "aware." Aware perhaps, that their "right," often is really just the side of fear—and perhaps so "fearfully right" that they cannot hear. And perhaps I'm only talking to dead air—perhaps.

With someone you love, that possibility is so hard to bear. And sometimes, we simply must let go: reach out instead, and touch those who love—those who will touch back—and nurture our souls with acceptance.

✶✶✶✶✶✶

See Life's Laws:
3   Thoughts are energy: Loving, or not loving (fear).
4   The energy out returns in kind.
5   For every sorrowful thing, there exists the potential for equal joy. The Universe always balances.

Questions and/or Exercises:
- **Is "right and wrong"** ultimately the peak for a mountain of dung dribbling out of the back end of a judgmental mind?
- **Speaking of** "dead air"—if your mind is locked into "right and wrong", the air around this last question won't smell very pleasant. So, is it?
- **If you do** smell the stink, don't you think you owe it to your soul, to search out the thoughts and beliefs that are its source and change them?

The Truth About Love

The need to feel loved is a basic human need. It is a need that cannot be filled outside oneself. Yet virtually all of Humanity has this need, for virtually no one has been taught to love themselves—and to put that love before all others.

To be humble in our society is an admirable thing. *We are taught* to look at ourselves as less than, and certainly not equal to others. *We are taught* to sacrifice ourselves because others are better and more deserving. *We are taught* to believe that our own life is not as worthy as another's.

Bottom line, *we are taught to be dysfunctional.* The truth is, we can only feel our own love. And without ever having felt it for ourselves, can we truly know love? No, nor can we have it to give to others. It is not that we need to feel loved, it is that we need to love ourselves, and then to feel ourselves loving others—and sometimes, to know that our love is returned.

******

See Life's Laws:
4	The energy out returns in kind.
22	We consciously only feel our own feelings.
12	Our lives are run by our needs, then by our wants.
15	One must do one's own thinking.
6	The energy of thoughts must flow.

Questions and/or Exercises:
- **Is love** an ego thing? Can it in any way be connected to the ego?
- **Is it** about being "better than?" Or is it just about "being?"
- **Is "being love"** something you have ever felt for yourself?
- **If not**—don't you know, you've yet to feel it for another? *Don't just answer "yes" or "no" here—write about it. And about how you feel about all those lies you have been taught.*

>>><<<

The Journey of the Heart

Commitment is only functional when it is to yourself. You *don't* know if you will always be with that other person, should there come a time when you—or they—don't want to be. You *do* know you will always be with yourself. The commitment part is about you loving you.

It is to commit to following your joy in life, and when you are with someone else, to loving them to the very best of your ability.

And if sometimes those joys should vary, and your paths depart, be committed to letting them go with love. It matters not what the other does; it is up to each to part with love—or not. This is when you each get to discover if your own love for them is real—and if theirs is also.

Commitment to love and to joy—to following your heart—is a personal journey. Your travel companions may change. But the love in your heart will not. If you loved them then, you will love them always—love is a forever thing.

Did you part with love—and did they? Perhaps they were in your life to give you this lesson about love—to show you if your love is the real deal. Maybe this is a lesson you gave to one another. The only things you need to consider are: Did *you* learn the lesson—did *you* learn how to love?

******

See Life's Laws:
21   Real love, once given, cannot be taken back.
10   The purpose of life is for those lessons.
8   The world is not "out there"—it is "in here."
18   Soul-to-soul pacts are made in the pre-existence.

Questions and/or Exercises:
- **If anyone** had hard feelings on parting, what does that tell you about them?
- **Was it** you?
- **Can real** love for you, ever depend on them doing, saying, or being, anything other than who they are?
- **If you** don't know within yourself what real love is, how can you ever know it, or accept it, when it is being given?

Living to Our Joy

If my mate won't live life to the joys that are hers alone, regardless of what I or others want, she's not living true to herself. If her life is a lie unto herself, how can it ever be otherwise to me? A lie is a lie. If it is something she says by way of convincing herself, the lie will show up expressed to me. Inside, she knows, and her life cannot go for long without expressing the truth.

Our true thoughts cannot help but create. It is a Spiritual Law: Thoughts create—always.

Wouldn't it be best to just live our lives to our own joys, restricting only those that are harmful to ourselves or others, and being aware of our own ego while ignoring the egos of others? Anyone whose ego is a stumbling block in my life doesn't belong there, for I give them this same courtesy.

My feelings are the messages from my soul, sent to tell me what I need to look at in order to grow. It is not my right to save others from their own feelings—from their own learning. And, I do consider it my duty to be honest with others about who I am.

Again, those who run their lives to suit their ego and expect us to run ours, to suit that same ego, don't belong in our lives—those of us who want to live in truth.

Sometimes that is a bitter truth to accept when it is about the person you love.

Still . . . A lie is a lie. The ego is the master of all liars. To become a liar, just to masturbate your loved one's ego—to make it feel good—where is there any love in that?

******

See Life's Laws:
2   Thoughts Create.
13   Our own life is our sole possession. Just so, it is for everyone.

Questions and/or Exercises:
- **Requiring** your mate to masturbate your ego may seem like fun. But the ensuing orgasm will make your relationship very sticky. Have you experienced it? *Write about it.*
- **There are** those who play the game of control and think it is love. Is this the bitter truth about the one you love? *Write about it—truthfully.*
- **Do you** understand that it is a demand they make of you, if you are to be allowed in their life?
- **Do you** know that to give in to that demand is to make a death wish to your soul? *Why is that?*

I'm Okay...

"I'm okay—you're all fucked-up." Such seems to be the lowest common denominator in the minds of many.

"In my life, I am better than you!" Perhaps we, in all our relationships, simply need to take another step in conscious evolution.

"I'm okay—for me. You're okay—for you. And, I see the love in you."

******

See Life's Laws:
13   Our own life is our sole possession. Just so, it is for everyone.
19   We are quintessentially beings of energy.
4   The energy out returns in kind.

Questions and/or Exercises:
- **It's none of** your business if others see you as "fucked-up." Only when you can accept it is their right—and not give a rats-ass—will they then have the opportunity to freely change their minds. *Surely you know someone who views you that way. Will you try it sincerely, in no way making it into a game of pretense?*
- **If that person** is your significant other, can you accept that you may be the only one in the relationship who evolves?

The Other Half of Loving is Accepting

A relationship is really only about needs and learning. Each person gets their own needs met, and each learning about themselves, in this great mirror called "a relationship." When the relationship is especially good, the needs met include the need to love. The learning in the mirror reflects the beauty of it. Yet for each, the relationship provides only the opportunity. It is about more than the giving, for each must also be willing to accept, and all in the space of honesty.

******

See Life's Laws:
9   Others are but a mirror for us to see ourselves.
6   The energy of thoughts must flow.

Questions and/or Exercises:
- **Is there** any need you have that you are afraid to express to your partner?
- **Are you** aware that it will bite you in the ass if you don't? ***Write about it.***
- **Do you** know that if you are "afraid", it is because you don't feel safe to be real and honest with them?
- **Do you** think they might have the same issues with you, about their own needs?
- **How can** you make your relationship a safe place for them to be?

Love and Acceptance

Love means a lot of different things to a lot of different people. But the bottom-line real truth about love is that it requires acceptance. It is a total thing—an all-out or nothing thing. This is why it requires acceptance.

Without acceptance, love is not love. It is simply a need
- the need for someone to be other than who they are with you.
- the need to control other people, because see them as being responsible for how we feel about everything.
- the need for you to believe in other people, because you don't believe in yourself.
- the need for you to look outside yourself, for someone who cares.
- the need for you to have someone else fill those gaps in you, where you are not there.

Without acceptance, there is simply a need. With acceptance, there is still a need—a need to give love. Real love is a giving thing, needing nothing outside of its giving.

******

See Life's Laws:
8   The world is not "out there"—it is "in here."
6   The energy of thoughts must flow.
13   Our own life is our sole possession. Just so, it is for everyone.
21   Real love, once given, cannot be taken back.

Questions and/or Exercises:
- **Do you** see that without acceptance, what most then see as being love, is only fear?
- **And those** needs mentioned?—Might they be the lies society has taught you to believe?

Driving a Relationship

Relationships are about the lessons. What drives them is your needs. For some, the relationship may have nothing to do with love. But likely most would agree; relationships are supposed to be about the need to give and receive love. Yet no matter what the needs may be, for relationships to work, the meeting of needs must exist for both. For when one's needs aren't met, they become the driving force in that person's life—the force that drives the relationship apart.

✶✶✶✶✶✶

See Life's Law:
12   Our lives are run by our needs, then our wants.

Questions and/or Exercises:
- **Is there** a force driving your relationship apart? If you don't know, then assume there is.
- **Is your** relationship a safe place for your partner to discuss his or her needs openly?
- **Do you** know that making it a safe place for you requires you first to make it so for them? *Write about it.*

Control Is Never Love

Having the courage to choose love in the face of that which is not, commands one's own respect.

That others cannot see it—others who would rather play that game of trying to control one another—others who would then try to convince themselves, by calling it love.

Yes, refusing to play that game takes courage, knowing you may no longer be accepted by those you love. And still, the fact remains that playing the game of control with someone you *"love"* is *never* loving.

******

See Life's Laws:
3   Thoughts are energy: Loving, or not loving (fear).
16   We only control ourselves.

Questions and/or Exercises:
- **How does** control raise its ugly little head in your own relationship?
- **Does it** too, spit at you if you don't submit—and doubly so, when you do?
- **Does it** show up as screaming-mee-mee fits of outrage—or just little insinuations of guilt?
- **In what** other ways has the game of control been played with you?—Or by you?

Giving

When you give of yourself—your love—to someone else, you are the one who gets the gift. You are the one who gets to feel your feelings.

******

See Life's Laws:
6   The energy of thoughts must flow.
22   We consciously only feel our own feelings.

Questions and/or Exercises:
- **Do you** think of it as being a special thing to love someone who accepts your love?
- **Is it then** required that they love you back?
- **If they** won't, would you still love them? This question, especially, will tell you loads about yourself and love—***don't screw yourself with a "yes" or "no" answer.***

No Freedom—No Love

As for me? I don't ever want to be in a relationship again where the lady is only staying because she feels she is stuck there by her marriage vows.

I want it to be that every time I look at her, I know that being with me is truly where she wants to be.

Let that bird free! Real love is to give one another that freedom.

Sure, I see things differently. To me, there is NO security in life. And yet, there are many who don't see it that way and spend a great deal of effort seeking it. I don't begrudge them their right to the elusive security of that false belief.

******

See Life's Laws:
8   The world is not "out there"—it is "in here."
3   Thoughts are energy: Loving, or not loving (fear).
16   We only control ourselves.

Questions and/or Exercises:
- **Do you** "get" that by making any demands on how you want another to be, you guarantee they won't show you the truth of who they are?
- **Would you** ever be okay with your significant other being with you if they don't want to be?
- **How can** you ever know if you try to control them in any way?
- **The only** thing that restricts freedom in your relationships is found in any price you might demand they pay. Do you see the need to make your relationship a "free to be yourself" place? *Write about it.*

The Way You Want It

For love to flourish, each must communicate, each must nourish. Each must be willing to look at—understand, and fulfill—the needs of the other. Yes, everyone has a belief system about love. Mine is not the same as yours. The trick is for me to tell you mine and to hear yours—then to give my love to you, in the way you want it.

If I cannot do that within the honest bounds of the joys of my soul, then it needs be that I take the lessons of you—the lessons of us—and move on.

And you? —We are each in this world with our own lives to live. What lessons you accept of me, are those you *want* to see—or maybe *need* to see—given you have the courage to look at all the private things I've told you. And I, to look at those things that are equally private to you, as mine are to me.

******

See Life's Laws:
9   Others are but a mirror for us to see ourselves.
18   Soul-to-soul pacts are made in the pre-existence.
12   Our lives are run by our needs, then our wants.
13   Our own life is our sole possession. Just so, it is for everyone.

Questions and/or Exercises:
- **"... those things that are equally private to you, as mine are to me."** Can you see that this is the whole crux of love/sexual relationships? They are about private things—things exposed and vulnerable!
- **You might** not have even understood it when you read it above. Did you?
- **It is** the reason I am going over this material repeatedly in different scenarios. Unless it is something dead-on personal, exactly like it is in their own life, some folks can't see it. Y'know?
- **The concept** of what real love is may be simple—the lies some folks tell about what they think love is are often complex. Can you see that? *Yup, you got it—write about it.*

Ultimatums

An ultimatum is the Hiroshima of control dramas. It is one person demanding that the other be different from who they are, in order to be acceptable. It is one saying, "I don't accept you being you." And a control drama, like all dramas, it is not love. So that person is also saying, "I don't love you."

Yeah, that one hits you like a nuclear bomb, doesn't it?

Ultimatums seldom sneak up on you like an unexpected fart. Unless a person is one hell of a control freak, they will never give you an ultimatum—not without repeatedly letting you know exactly what it is about you, that is unacceptable to them. An ultimatum is the ultimate in the selfish pursuit of trying to change you to suit them.

The fallout from an ultimatum is deadly to a relationship.

******

See Life's Laws:
3   Thoughts Are Energy: *Love, or not love (fear)*
13   Our own life is our sole possession. Just so, it is for everyone.
16   We Only Control Ourselves.
21   Real Love, Once Given, Cannot Be Taken Back
26   Change Requires The Truth of One's Heart.

Questions and/or Exercises:
➢ **If you** truly wanted to be the person they are demanding you to be, wouldn't you have already become that person?
➢ **Can you** see that for you, to make an unwanted change for them, would be for you both to live a lie—an unsustainable lie?
➢ **Do you** really want to become a liar, pretending to be someone whom they can pretend to love?
➢ **Do you** want a relationship based on a struggle to control, or one based on love?
➢ **Isn't it** clear, you can't have both? *Write down your thoughts—don't whimp out on yourself with yes or no answers.*

>>><<<

The Relationship Game

Don't like the games being played in your relationship—the drama—the control?

Then you must become aware that you are in the game—and that control is never love, rather, always fear. You are playing your own part in it—and you can stop. Then the relationship will either stop or change. You are the creator of the game you play—or don't play.

Most continue to play, only out of fear of what they will lose if they stop. Never being aware of the love one gains in not playing the game of control, and in having a relationship with a person, also not playing.

Will that person be the same person you are playing with now? That depends on whether they are more enamored with the fearful illusion of control—something they are currently very familiar with—or, if they have the capacity to change to something they do not know: *real love*.

******

See Life's Laws:
13   Our own life is our sole possession. Just so, it is for everyone.
3   Thoughts are energy: Loving, or not loving (fear).
4   The energy out returns in kind.
5   For every sorrowful thing, there exists the potential for equal joy. The Universe always balances.

Questions and/or Exercises:
- **The only** question you truly have the right to consider is: Do *you* have that capacity?
- **Have you** been following—do you understand the concept yet of what real love is—or would you rather play the game of control?
- **If so,** what part in the game do you play? *What do you think about all this?*

>>><<<

Giving and Accepting

Your life is not about anyone but yourself—and then, there are relationships. That is where stuff gets really fuzzy. It might help to remember this: It is not what your mate gives to the relationship, but rather what you accept from it, that is the limiting factor—for you.

To grow your life in a relationship, both must give and both must accept. You may do your life together, but it is still about yourself. You're just adding the option of loving someone else.

******

See Life's Laws:
13   Our own life is our sole possession. Just so, it is for everyone.
19   We are quintessentially beings of energy.
22   We consciously only feel our own feelings.

Questions and/or Exercises:
- **Does your** significant other give you the option of loving him or her?
- **Do you** accept love from him or her?
- **Can you** see that a loving relationship cannot exist if both parties do not give as well as receive?
- **Why do** you think I use the term "won't" instead of "can't?" *(Can't give a one-word answer here, can you? And no, the "f-bomb" is two words. Maybe it ought to be, but it doesn't stand for "fun bomb)." It's okay. I know, about all this ooey-gooey—heart on your sleeve, talk about your real feelings stuff. A lot of folks won't handle it. Yup. There I go with that "won't" shit again. The point here is to get real—those of you who haven't already.*

Diamonds

It's really easy to fall in love with a diamond. But a diamond is still just a rock. How much does a rock love you back? Know of anyone you think of as being a diamond? Could it be that they, too, are incapable of loving you back? —Or is it that you are incapable of seeing the beauty beyond the glitter?

Wow! That last thing gives a whole different take on why they might be incapable of loving you back—do you think?

Then again, you might ask yourself. "If it is only about glitter, can there be any real love going on here?"

******

See Life's Laws:
3   Thoughts are energy: Loving, or not loving (fear).
22   We consciously only feel our own feelings.
21   Real love, once given, cannot be taken back.

Questions and/or Exercises:
- Well, **IS** your relationship only about the glitter?
- **Do you** love them only for their looks?
- **Do you** think your own looks are what make you loveable?
- **Or is the** glitter about how much money they—or you— have? *Write about it.*

Relationships—Needs & Soul Mates

Relationships are simply about growing and providing one another with the lessons we need to grow, lessons that will be beaten out—forged—over the anvil of our needs.

The difference between having a regular relationship and having that ultimate one, some call a "soul mate," is simply that soul mates don't go kicking and screaming when it comes to learning the lessons we provide for them.

As for that "anvil of your needs?" Soul mates won't break your anvil and go screaming into the night. Besides, for the most part, your needs are simply what it takes to know your own heart. With a soul mate, the learning is non-judgmental and easy.

And the rest? Everything else in life is just wants.

******

See Life's Laws:
8   The world is not "out there"—it is "in here."
7   Blame is the abdication of responsibility.
9   Others are but a mirror for us to see ourselves.
18   Soul-to-soul pacts are made in the pre-existence.
10   The purpose of life is for those lessons.
21   Real love, once given, cannot be taken back.

Questions and/or Exercises:
- **Do you** resist learning the lessons your mate provides?
- **Do you** ever try to change them rather than accept the lesson?
- **Has either** one ever gone screaming into the night?
- **If so, was** it in search of someone who won't give you that lesson—or was it to crawl back at daybreak, asking for that same lesson all over again?
- **If any** of these questions apply to you, wouldn't it be easier to just learn the lesson? *Yep, write about it.*

Soul Mates

Love is being a companion.

Love is giving your companion the freedom to be exactly who they are, without penalty.

Love is in knowing there is nothing for which you will need to forgive them. No matter what they do, you will always see the spiritual being they are and love them.

Yes, you can always have a loving relationship, but the loving part must happen on your own side. It does not always happen equally on their side. Those things they do may eventually become a deal-breaker for your relationship. Forgiving them just means you accept them and don't hold them as being wrong in your own mind. It does not mean it works for you. If you truly love them, you will part with love, wishing them well and nothing less.

The truth is, you can love someone that you do not want to be with. And likely, it is only because your love is not being returned, in the same manner and measure it is given—the energy of your love does not match. You are not mentally and/or spiritually matched.

Spiritually? Love happens on a spiritual plane. Relationships happen on this, the physical plane. Soul mates happen only when these planes are a match for both. What most on this physical plane think of as love is more likely to be fearful need.

And mentally? That's about the conscious physical plane. Let's take that answer to the extreme. If your partner wants to have sex with other people, that must be something you are okay with—if you are mentally matched. Tough order—finding someone with the kind of courage to be that honest. Even tougher for them to find someone with that kind of acceptance.

Funny thing, the last statistic I heard was that cheating covers about 60% of married men and 40% of wives. Too bad people cannot always be honest about their sexuality. The 20% of women left over would then have no valid excuse to blame anyone but themselves—and 40% of all men and women could be having a great time swinging. Of the 40% who are monogamously faithful, hopefully they will stay that way—or at least be honest if they don't. But then, maybe the 20% of those ladies blindsided and pissed-off (and divorced) can then become lesbians to even up the score—hell, maybe that is where some lesbians actually come from. I dunno.

What does all this say about honesty? Can there be any question that dishonesty is the cock-blocker to everything "relationship?" Without honesty, one can never know who the other is. *You have nothing, if either of what you give and what you get is not honest—double that "nothing" if it is the same with your partner.*

******

See Life's Laws:
21   Real love, once given, cannot be taken back.
16   We only control ourselves.
22   We consciously only feel our own feelings.

Questions and/or Exercises:
- **I used** sex for the "mentally matched" example, because sex is where relationships get hung up the most. Has cheating ever happened by you, or to you?
- **Are you** spiritually and mentally matched with your mate?
- **You cannot** know that if you both have not been honest—have you? Honesty starts with you.

- **Do you** have honesty in your relationship? That is not to say you or they, haven't made mistakes—which brings up the question of acceptance.
- **Are you** both free to be exactly who you are—ALWAYS? *Yes, there's a lot to write about here.*
- It might help to keep in mind that sex is NOT LOVE. Do you really think that cheating ever happens when there is real love?
- Is it possible that they cheated with someone else, because there was a need that they couldn't be honest with you about?
- Relationships are about the meeting of needs. If you really loved one another, you'd want them to have their needs met.
- Your choice would then be to accept it, maybe even join in and enjoy it. Or to appreciate their honesty and part from them with love.

Lovegasm

Unhealthy people fall in love to fill the emptiness—the missing needs that they mistake as somehow being "not whole." They attempt to find someone *"out there"* to fill it, for the needs are most always about love.

Healthy people are those who have looked within themselves for the love they need for themselves, and finding it, fill themselves to overflowing. Once there is such an abundance on the inside, they then look to someone *"out there"* to whom to give it.

When they find someone of equal abundance, only then can love blossom past simple need, to the full fruition of a "lovegasm."

******

See Life's Laws:
6   The energy of thoughts must flow.
8   The world is not "out there"—it is "in here."
12   Our lives are run first by our needs, then our wants.
3   Thoughts are energy: loving, or not loving (fear).

Questions and/or Exercises:
- **Do you** understand that this is the first step you take on the path to your soul mate?
- **Do you** believe that love begins from inside or outside ourselves?
- **Could those** described as "healthy" ever get that way except by choosing the energy of love in their daily life, instead of fear?
- **Perhaps the** real question you need to answer here is: Given those as described above, where do you fit in—healthy or unhealthy? *Why?*

>>><<<

Working At A Relationship

It is not true that you have to "work at a relationship". You just have to work at the lessons—the lessons concerning you that the other person is providing. Concentrating on the lessons is the hard part.

Learning to accept the other, *exactly as they are,* is always one of your hardest lessons. It's much easier to focus on fixing and changing—that struggle to control one another. That fearful lesson that keeps you in the space of fear when what you want is to love.

The struggle to control, coupled with unacceptance, both are fear energies that leave little room in a relationship for real love. Most are oblivious to the truth, seeing that struggle AS ACTUALLY BEING what most couples call love—sad.

※※※※※※

See Life's Laws:
9   Others are but a mirror for us to see ourselves.
10   The purpose of life is for those lessons.
18   Soul-to-soul pacts are made in the pre-existence.

Questions and/or Exercises:
- **What does** the term "work at a relationship" mean to you?
- **Is it about** dealing with what you dislike about them—about trying to make compromises with each other, in order to be acceptable companions?
- **When each** has to change something about themselves that they don't want to change, can either have what they want?
- **Wouldn't it** then be a lose/lose situation?
- **You changing** your perception to seeing them as acceptable—exactly as they are—would that not help them to see you the same way?

>>><<<

A Single Man's Prayer

Lord save me from the "religious" woman! For if her God is the source of all joy in her life, guess who gets to be responsible for all her pain.

Thank you, God, for the power in the knowledge given by the Spiritual Law: *"I am the Creator"*—that *we* are *one* with the power of the Universe. And my connection with that power creates everything in my life.

Given a physical attraction, some special joys in common, and a woman who is also the sole creator of her life, then there is no limit to the joy we will create together, *one* together with *You!*

Namaste' Lord . . .

    Namaste'.

See Life's Laws:
1   I am the creator.
20   We are part of the energy that comprises God.
7   Blame is the abdication of responsibility.

Questions and/or Exercises:
- **You would** have to accept and understand these "Laws of Life" in order to understand what this one is saying. Do you? If not, it's okay to come back at a later time and re-read. *The exercise here is to put this one in your own words.*

>>><<<

Fearful Needs

The experience of true love between two people never results in pain. Pain between lovers is always the direct result of fear—those unmet fearful needs within themselves!

******

See Life's Laws:
4   The energy out returns in kind.
12   Our lives are run first by our needs, then our wants.
21   Real love, once given, cannot be taken back.

Questions and/or Exercises:
- **Is there** pain in your life because you loved someone and they left you?
- **If death** took them away, why is it that you can't honor them by remembering them without the pain?
- **In fact**, no matter the reason they left, why is it you can't honor them with the joy of your own love?
- **Honoring** someone who has left you requires you to truly love them—love as in, then *and* now. True love, once given, is forever. *Write down your thoughts on this.*
- **Can you** see that the pain of a missing loved one is always a selfish thing caused only by your inability to accept "what is" in life?

In the End

Love? It's not how you feel about someone you've just met, someone with whom you are starting a relationship. The *truth* is about how you feel when it has ended.

Doesn't matter what has happened in the meantime—all that doesn't mean *shit*. Fact is, if you don't love them and wish them the very best in the end, *then you never loved them at all.*

******

See Life's Law:
21   Real love, once given, cannot be taken back.

Questions and/or Exercises:
- **Have you** ever had an ex whom you now harbor harsh feelings toward?
- **If so,** wouldn't it be wise to think hard on this reflection?
- **It is** never too late to change your mind—not if you're still alive—y'know?

Exercise: Let's look at what your needs were that drove your relationship.

For you guys:
Were you just lonely and wanted some enjoyable sexual company?
Did you need a servant—someone to keep the house clean, cook, and wash the skid marks out of your shorts?
Did you want someone who looked up to you and would put up with your shit?

Now ladies:
Was he only there to provide you security in life?
Did you want to be one of his possessions?
Did you need to have someone who appreciated the care you took of him?

Now for you both:
If you cheated, what was the need that the other wasn't meeting?
Why was it they couldn't be honest with you about it?

Perfect Love

Finding that one perfect love is not about the perfection of that other person, but rather the perfection of your own love.

The love you find is always the one the Creator sends to give you the lessons you need to learn. If it ends with your anger, then you failed the lesson. Try again until you do learn. Therin lies the perfection.

See Life's Laws:
8   The world is not "out there"—it is "in here."
4   The energy out returns in kind.
22   We consciously only feel our own feelings.

Questions and/or Exercises:
- **Do you** think that love is something that the other person gives to you—or is it something you give to them?
- **Given that** most believe it is both, which one do you think you have control over?
- **Which one** do you not?
- **Is it possible** that the one you control is the love that needs to be your sole concern?
- **There is** only one person on earth that you can truly control. Who is that? *Write about it.*

The Flashbulb of Love

When the flashbulb of fresh love goes off in your face, sometimes you trip over things in your way—things you don't see. Sometimes they are things you put there, then don't look at. Always, there is a dazzling haze left in the backlash of that flash, which hides the picture.

You determine how long that haze will last. Some couples stumble through life in that haze together, forever. Others learn from the pain of their falls, look at their self-imposed obstacles, and gain the true gift of insight.

With insight comes the ability to run, to move faster and further in one's life. Sometimes the gift is accepted by only one, whose heart then cries, as it is carried away by life.

******

See Life's Laws:
10 The purpose of life is for those lessons.
9   Others are but a mirror for us to see ourselves.
14 Change is the constant of the Universe.

Questions and/or Exercises:
- **Is it** possible that the other person was just in your life to teach you things about yourself?
- **Things that** for your soul to "know," you had to experience?
- **Can you** accept the "gift" of it and move on in life with gratitude?
- **Is it possible** it may not be the same experience for them?
- **That they** may not need this same "gift?"

>>><<<

Sex Is A Beautiful Thing

Let's talk the nitty-gritty about SEX—the physical act. Doesn't matter if it is love making—or FUCKING. Either way, it is a beautiful thing, and, as one ages, it WILL change.

Some women will lose their sexual "want to." Some men will lose their "ability to." I've heard it said that ED (erectile dysfunction) happens to 70% of men at some point. I think that figure is lower than the truth.

I hope you women never have to face the following situation, but consider this: Some women get breast cancer and end up losing one or more breasts. Yes, assuming they survive, it is still a personal disaster—especially with their viewpoint of how they see themselves as a woman. It's no different from a man with ED. For both, it is nothing short of a catastrophe!

And then, there is the bottom line of all sexual love—and all straight out fucking. That being each person is giving the gift of it to the other, helping one another meet their need for sexual release. Women can take the hormones they may be lacking, and/or get their breasts rebuilt. A man can acquire toys, and, in turn, he can develop his oral skills.

But my point is that it is also a gift when each is able to help the other see themselves as a functional being once again—yeah, maybe even a sexual dynamo.

Disaster? Hell, look to the upside. A woman can have bigger, perkier breasts than she could otherwise, given the realities of aging. A man can give his woman a variety, or maybe just the exact size, shape, and feel of her preferred dick, and can make it a variety of acts lasting throughout her ability to have multiple orgasms.

That's not to mention that he can develop his taste buds for sexual cuisine. In the process, each is giving the gift of sex, and for the one, a gift concerning their personal viewpoint in how they view themselves as a sexual being.

One of life's simple truths is Spiritual Law #56—
Sex is not love. It is a need.

Ah, yes, no matter how many orgasms a man may provide to her, in her perception, few women can separate sex and orgasms from man-meat. They somehow must go together to fulfill her need.

And for a guy, fulfilling her need may then require an adjustment in his own perception—given they both want to remain together. It all boils down to loving her enough to change his perception from what society says is "wrong" to what you both know is her need.

And you both have the power to change your perception, if you truly love one another, which brings us once again to one of society's—especially religious society's—most dysfunctional lies.

The truth lies in the Spiritual Law #32—
There is no "good or bad," no "right or wrong."
It is all God—God's love or humanity's fear.

If you truly do love them, you will do what is needed. You can be okay, encouraging them to get their sexual needs met in an open/honest manner by someone who can and wants to. Yeah, that's right: it's called an "open" relationship, and it can work for you.

You can even do it as a "Hot Wife" situation as a threesome together. Or even as a "Cuckold," without his participation and/or hopefully without her need to demean him.

There are options in a changing mature relationship. You—each person reading this—can make those golden years even better sexually than the BEST years you ever had while moaning with those raging hormones of youth, again, if you have love enough.

******

See Life's Law:
   The ones you need to consider most are already mentione

Questions and/or Exercises:
- **If sex is** an issue, will you approach your partner for an honest solution?
- **If he can't** satisfy you as a man, then as a woman, can you accept his male lesbian alternatives to the reality of "man-meat," and possibly even enjoy those alternatives more?"
- **If you** have a problem with either of the above questions, is it possible you have love and ego mixed?
- **Your perception** is your reality. You have the ability to change it at will. Will you?
- **Man or woman**, do you now look at aging and sexuality differently?
- **Two of society's** most horrific lies are mentioned. Can you see the truth yet?
- **Do you** realize how truly fucked up our societies have been to the health of our species?
- **Will you** endeavor to raise your children in the truth and/or teach them better if they are now adults?
- **You do** know that the best way to change others is by your example—right?

In the Energy

In the energy of life, there is only *love* or what is not love—*fear*. (Yeah, I'm still harping on law #3.)

To be in a relationship, just because both want to be there—that's about *love*. And it's also about *freedom,* as either has the freedom not to be together, if it's not where they want to be.

To have a relationship where either one demands promises or legal chains, that's *not* love, not the pure freedom of *love;* rather, that's *fear*. It cannot be stressed enough that there can be no *love* when there is *fear*

******

See Life's Law:
3 Thoughts are energy: Loving, or not loving (fear).
4 The energy out returns in kind.
17 What we hold with energy runs our lives.
19 We are quintessentially beings of energy.
16 We only control ourselves.
21 Real love, once given, cannot be taken back.
22 We consciously only feel our own feelings.
23 Now is the only time there is.

Questions and/or Exercises:
> **Do you** think just maybe, we are talking about marriage—not that there can't be real love in a marriage? But marriage *is* one of society's lies: If you are in love, you get married—right? A few will oblige out of habit, not because they need promises and chains. Society's lie only protects those who are lying about being in love—such protection is required, for when the other finds that out. *Write about it*

- block to real love?
- **The freedom in** real love does not speak to the freedom to "sexually cheat." If there is dishonesty, can there ever be real love?
- **Cheating is NOT about fucking other people, it IS about the dishonesty**. *Write about this too.*
- **Monogamy may be required by one or both, and like marriage, it is then about fear. Monogamy may be a mutual option, but it is not a requirement of love. In fact, as a requirement by either person, it is a cockblock to love.**

Saying It With Love

There's nothing wrong with you. And there's nothing wrong with me—

It's not even about anyone being wrong. It's just that together—you and me—there's something that . . . just . . . doesn't . . . work.

Our worlds are comprised of how we see life. And our worlds—yours and mine—are just too far apart.

******

See Life's Laws:
7   Blame is the abdication of responsibility.
13   Our own life is our sole possession. Just so, it is for everyone.

Questions and/or Exercises:
> **The above** is an example of rejecting someone's advances with love. Do you see how it is simply about accepting "what is" without blame? *How could you do it better? If you can think of other loving ways, write about them. This is something you will want to think about now.*

F.U.C.K.

The word is from a mid-fifteenth-century English acronym: For Unlawful Carnal Knowledge. But in whose mind was such a God-given natural thing, so piously labeled as carnal—a puritan term of the time meaning sinful? And who was the control freak who made it unlawful? How many minds were damaged by banning such knowledge? Wouldn't it have been so much more nurturing to mankind, had the acronym instead been: For Un-judgmental Connecting Kindness?

Be that so—or not. And some do claim it is not. But then, they're probably just the down-in-the-mouth fans of the rock group Van Halen.

******

See Life's Law:
4   The energy out returns in kind.
3   Thoughts are energy: Loving, or not loving (fear).

Questions and/or Exercises:
- **Do you** see how many of our unconscious beliefs originated from some shit-for-brains asshole from way back when?
- **Are we** now the current irresponsible assholes who unconsciously keep passing those beliefs down to our own children?
- **It's no** longer about anyone's fault—still, don't you think we owe it to them to become more conscious? *Write about it.*

Grit Your Teeth and Buck Up

The previous reflection, *"Saying it with Love,"* is about telling you the full truth. Remember the one titled *Omissions*— found in the front of both Books One and Two. You are about to find out why I put something some might see as unimportant, right in your face, first thing.

You see, everything worth having comes with a price. The universe always balances, and *there is a price* to seeing your world differently from most of society. I warned you that change takes courage, and some things in this book would not feel good.

So grit your teeth and buck up—
These Spiritual Laws —*The Laws of Truth*—will give you a more functional, enjoyable world to live in, but that world, remember, is "in here."

What most others see as being "the world" is still "out there." We all share life, and living yours to the truth of Spiritual Law will still be functional between you and them. Your interactions with others will be peaceful—theirs with you may not be so.

That does not change about those who see the world "out there." You'll find you can see things about them and their lives that they cannot, and that your reactions to life in general will be different from theirs, from what yours once were. Well and good.

Where most go when you don't live your life to suit their own is drama and control. And they'll demand that you be responsible for their choice of feelings. For most living "out there," it is a simple acknowledgment of their feelings, that is all you need to do—*"I'm so sorry you feel that way...."*

It is your relationship with a significant other that will change—yeee-up, you've got it—*significantly*. The standard relationship usually involves a lot of control—each demanding the other be responsible for how they, themselves, choose to feel, then arguing and fighting until one accepts that lie, and gives control over to the other.

Then there exists a win/lose relationship, unless both are determined to win, making it a constant lose/lose relationship.

The drama of control isn't love and doesn't leave much room for love—it doesn't leave *any* room, if it's a constant thing. This is what love is like with those who won't take responsibility for their own life and for their own choice of feelings.

If you accept this book, you'll begin seeing life from the view given by these Laws. You become the creator of your life and take responsibility for it, and for your feelings about it all—works for you.

But it will blow your significant other out of the water—they cannot be the winner in that struggle if you are no longer playing the game. Some will see the changes in you and like them. They may even take this same journey. But it is one that you cannot make them take— (Law 13).

This road you're now on has a fork, and for most couples, it comes unexpectedly. Each must decide which path they want to take. Life is your personal soul's journey. Yours may well part at this fork— key word "well," because your soul calls the shots here. This fork is the omission most teachers of spiritual law leave out.

I do not. This is the price some pay to be the creator of their lives. If you are single—or if your significant other has taken that other fork—you may want to keep handy the previous reflection—*Saying it With Love*. It may be useful for a time, before another loving, enlightened soul becomes your partner on this journey.

✶✶✶✶✶✶

See Life's Laws:
1	I am the creator.
5	For every sorrowful thing, there exists the potential for equal joy. The Universe always balances.
8	The world is not "out there"—it is "in here."
13	Our own life is our sole possession. Just so, it is for everyone.

Questions/exercises to consider:
- **The cost** is great, but the gain is equally so. Would you rather I didn't tell you about *this* cost?
- **Have you** received your invitation from your significant other to play the game of control? It goes something like this: ***"I'm okay, you're all fucked-up."*** Are you still playing?
- **You do** know that in declining, there can be but one answer? ***"I'm so sorry you feel that way."***
- **You do** know how that answer usually results in one action on your part? What is that?
- **To stave** off the pain of it requires you to do this first: Accept his/her right to be who they are and love them anyway—before you leave. Will you, or have you, done that?
- **Do you** understand that there is someone waiting—someone who will understand you, accept you, and love you, exactly for who you are? And you cannot meet them until you are beyond your pain?
- **I don't** mean to scare you off—and then, there are those lies of omission I said I wouldn't tell. And I've told you about this price before—it's just that some listen with their head. I'm hoping this time you're listening with your heart. Do you understand that my personal integrity is on the line?
- **Do you** know that I've been here also—and survived? ***"I am so sorry this cannot be a feelie-good book. It is the price of your freedom, from the lies."*** Write about it all.

>>><<<

Book Two
PART FOUR

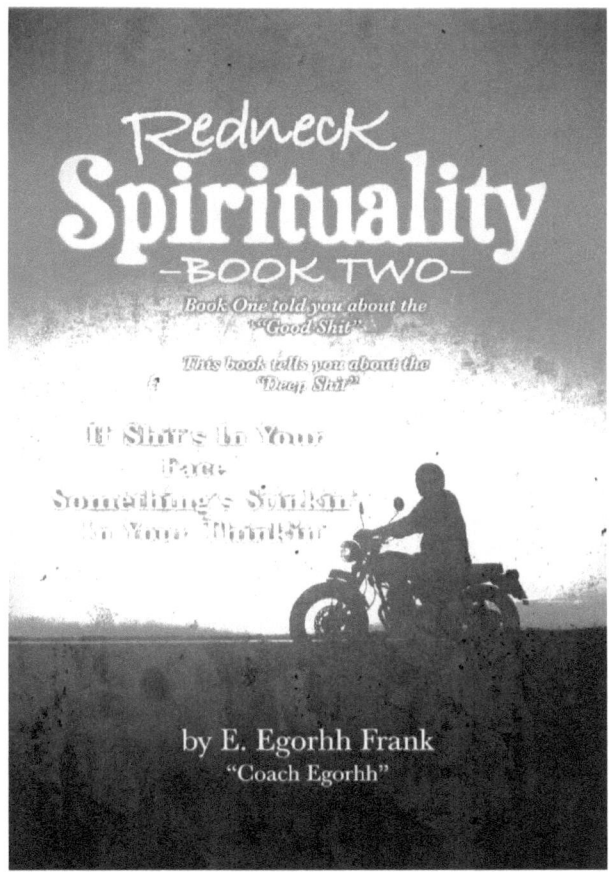

About Politics
In The Light of The Laws

The Collective Consciousness

One must always be aware that lumping everyone together most often results in a disservice. Thing is, with some aspects of life, there is a collective consciousness. Such it is in politics

What people do is to look to those who think similarly and to lump themselves into that thinking. That's what politics does. Given that there are those who think lovingly and those who don't. Their thinking supports your own—and when your thinking is not loving, you know it. But they then support that unloving part of you. Politics encourages one to be as unloving as one wants, especially when carried to extremes.

It seems recently, both parties have been gravitating to extremes. That we have a two-party system makes it difficult to be loving and independent. It is the extremes of each party that we consider the unloving parts.

The general ideology of each in recent years is reaching a tipping point. One party now lends itself more to those unloving extremists than the other. This is expressed in its actions.

The truth of one's thinking is ALWAYS expressed
in one's actions.

The following is not so much about Democrats or Republicans, but rather is based on their actions. It is about the unequal extremes—and about power. Politics in general IS about power.

✶✶✶✶✶✶

See Life's Laws:
15—In a functional life, one must do one's own thinking.
8—The world is not "out there"—it is "in here."
17—The energy to which we hold fast is what runs our lives.
4—The energy out returns in kind.

Questions and/or Exercises:
- **Is your** thought system one of extremes?
- **Do you** fit into the extreme end of either party?
- **What are** the things you dislike about your party?
- **Are they** loving or unloving things? *Write.*

Which Side of the Fence

"If you ever wondered what side of the fence you sit on, this is a great test. I wish I could tell you who wrote it, but the copy I had was unsigned. In general, I agree with what is said.

If a conservative doesn't like guns, he doesn't buy one.
If a liberal doesn't like guns, he wants all guns outlawed.

If a conservative is a vegetarian, he doesn't eat meat.
If a liberal is a vegetarian, he wants all meat products banned for everyone.

If a conservative is down and out, he thinks about how to better his situation.
A liberal wonders who is going to take care of him.

If a conservative doesn't like a talk show host, he switches channels.
Liberals demand that those they don't like be shut down.

If a conservative is a non-believer, he doesn't go to church.
A liberal non-believer wants all mention of God and Jesus silenced.

If a conservative decides he needs health care, he goes about shopping for it, or may choose a job that provides it.
A liberal demands that the rest of us pay for his."

Anonymous Author

Left Turn—Right Turn—

Yes, this is not a feelie-good workbook, and there are some who argue that politics breaks with the general theme of this book. It does not. This —Book Two—takes it all a step deeper in asking the questions about which many don't want to get honest. The question of politics is only one, and we haven't even come to Organized Religions and their God, vs. Spirituality, and its Higher Power—yet. This book is about looking at yourself—and about honesty. You have what you have—you are who you are. What doesn't work in your life will never change unless you can see the truth and apply it to yourself with honesty. Soon, there will be a Book Three. It will deal with the real stinky stuff—our shit.

And truth?—I suggest you look to the Spiritual Laws, and not the lies of society, politics, or religion. The Spiritual Laws—these Laws of Life—are exactly that: the truth. They are not something this author made up.

These "in-depth" subjects all concern power. Where and how is power used—or misused?

•There is the power government gives a politician over his/her constituents by virtue of the laws and use of those laws.

•There is a like power that religion gives to the preacher by use of the power his/her congregation perceives is wielded by that preacher, supposedly in the name of God.

•In relationships, there is the power one gives to the other concerning the vulnerabilities of the heart.

•In all cases where power is involved, there will be those who will abuse it—teachers, bosses, corporate leaders, spouses, etc.

They use that power to raise someone up, or put someone down—a use determined by whether the wielder lives life in the energy of love or fear. Sadly, where power is concerned, those who are loving don't need or want power. And few of those who do want power will want to look at who they themselves become while wielding it.

This is one reason why this redneck book is so "in your face, down and dirty." Nearly everyone alive at some time is involved with the wielding of power. But this book is not asking you to look at others. It is about asking you to look at yourself.

See Life's Laws:
3 Thoughts are energy: Loving, or not loving (fear)
4 The energy out, returns in kind.

Exercise:
- ➢ **Write about** all the places you see power used. Is it used lovingly, or un-lovingly?
- ➢ **Then take** it home to where, and in what energy, you use power. Was any of it used lovingly—look again. Some believe that control is necessary. I agree—when it is about protecting myself or loved ones from physical harm.
- ➢ **Outside of** that, can attempting to control another adult ever be loving?
- ➢ **For me,** control over another is never wanted, and seldom needed. *What about you—yeah, write about it?*

Liberals, Conservatives, and Spiritual Laws

Liberals want to demand that the way they see life—and create theirs—must be the same for you. And they want to use the strong arm of government to make it so.

Conservatives take responsibility for their own lives—and only their own. They want to use their government's strong arms only to keep themselves safe from those others who would actually do them physical harm.

Liberals believe that how they see life as being, must be the same way you see it, too. They want to use government to physically control your life—and your mind? They want control of that too—but not their own.

Conservatives don't give a shit about what you think; they only care about what you do. They want no control over you except when you are being injurious to themselves.

With Liberals, whatever the means is okay, because they know what's best for you.

Conservatives only want the freedom to control themselves.

✶✶✶✶✶✶

See Life's Laws:
1   I am the creator.
7   Being the creator requires responsibility.
13   Our own life is our sole possession. Just so, it is for everyone.

Questions and/or Exercises:
- ➢ Who do you think is more functional and why?
- ➢ When it comes to loving others, which group is the more loving? Why?
- ➢ Which group is most apt to be telling themselves lies in order to get what they want? Why?
- ➢ Is that because the laws they live by—precepts—of their lives are lies?
- ➢ In which group do you think you belong? And why?
- ➢ These thoughts are only in general. Some of us refuse to allow those on the far side to push us equally far to either side. We attempt ot see truth and reason. Where do you stand in the cesspool known as politics?

Repeating History

It has been said:
Those who cannot remember the past are condemned to repeat it.
—George Santayana
History doesn't repeat itself, but it does rhyme.
—Mark Twain

So let's look at Hitler. He built his following upon the ideals of an "Elite Aryan Race." Then he invited all those working-class, wanna-be elitists to bully the rest of the German population into submission. Lastly, he gave them all someone to hate—the Jews.

Sound familiar? Look at our 2016 Presidential election. One side is constantly accusing the other of everything they themselves are saying, doing, and being. In a shark tank full of political lies, who's to say what the truth is? Near as I can see, only one side has employed wanna-be bully-boys, and yet tried to label the other as being another "Hitler"—all the while considering themselves as being the real elite class.

So I have to ask myself: Did America dodge a bullet with the results of this election? Seems so, those "elite" losers now are refusing to accept the will of the people, and are making the winners into their target to hate? What will it take to bring us all back together as Patriotic Americans?

Will it take ISIS becoming that hateful target?—Or North Korea?—Or Iran? Can we Americans survive our stupidity—our unwillingness to get real about ourselves?

Why are we so bent on victimizing ourselves with hate?

Bottom line: *Hate* is the reaction side of *fear*. And *fear* is not *love*. We don't have to lie down and become victims of any of it. Outside of threatening you or your life physically, no one can make you a victim but you. And, what with this socialist nonsense, my way of life—our whole society—is indeed being threatened. So how can I resist being their victim?

Resisting through arms, which the 2nd Amendment gives us the ability to do, is one choice—the fearful choice of last resort. No, my choice is to squeal like a hog. When others hear me and start to think for themselves, they too will start squealing, and the takeover of our way of life can be stopped.

Squealing may sound like a victim, but the true victims are those whose heads are buried in the sand. I chose to resist all that *fear*, but to resist it in the space of *love*. When others see me loving myself by refusing to be a victim, perhaps they too will choose to join in—and still others will then follow. And it is not even about *me*—It is simply a choice between *love* and *fear*. And I would love to see my government cleaned up by the simple squealing of a hog—one whose head is not buried in the sand, and whose ass is then, no longer presented for the porking.

Taking offense with others when it is only over our own poor choice of feelings is senseless. Taking offense at others who threaten us physically is necessary.

―――― ― ― ― ――――

See Life's Laws:
3   Thoughts are energy: Loving, or not loving (fear).
4   The energy out, returns in kind.
8   The world is not "out there"—it is "in here."

Questions and/or Exercises:
- **If you** are a hard-working sweat hog—like I spent my life being—do you believe it's your duty to feed those who won't work?
- **Or are** you one of those hogs being fed at the public trough, who keep voting in those dishonest politicians who are buying your vote?
- **Do you** respect yourself enough to work, and love yourself enough not to allow others to run your life?
- **Some bury** their heads in the sand and keep quiet. Who do you know who would unseemly squeal, rather than accept being a victim?
- **List them.** *Are you on the list?*

>>><<<

Book Two
PART FIVE

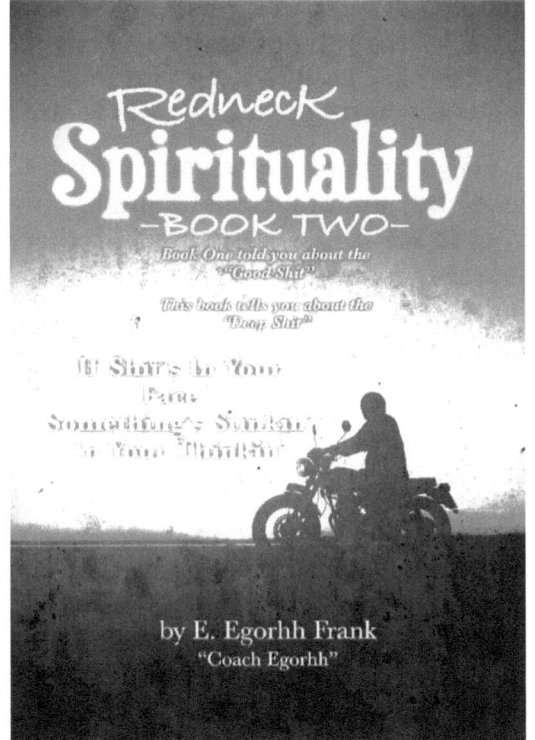

Organized Religion, Spirituality, and a Higher Power
In The Light of The Laws

NOTE:

Most examples concerning religion are written from a Judeo-Christian standpoint. They are generally valid for other religions, as most are in the "organized" category. Where this book is concerned, it holds that there exists a "higher power."

And about that higher power, the word most used to recognize it is "GOD." But problems arise in that we mere mortals have generally been indoctrinated by the use of blinders. Like a mule pulling the wagon of life, blinders are used to keep that mule focused. And the focus with religions is whatever each chooses to use to define God.

In other words, religions don't want you to think for yourself—or to get distracted by unauthorized thoughts. Most Christian religions want you to see God as a "being," up there somewhere in a place called Heaven, and apart from you.

For you to be in God's presence requires you to go to one of God's houses, where your connection is somehow dependent on the preacher. Some even require you to be on your knees. Is that out of respect for God, or to the preacher—or does it just make it easier to pick your pocket?

Enough with the "blasphemous" jokes. For some, this writing will likely rip those blinders right off their virgin minds. When this book says "God," it really means much more than what those blinders ever allowed anyone to see—ah, the bright light of truth, shining into an awakened mind. In writing this book, I was tempted to use the word "SOURCE" in place of "GOD." But it takes time for folks to see beyond what their "organized religions" have for so long allowed. Even with blinders the light can be dazzling.

Again:

This is NOT a feely-good book.

The Ocean of God

**I am but a drop
in the Ocean of God.
Not greater than . . .
Not less than . . .
Just the same as . . .
The whole.**

******

See Life's Laws:
20   We are part of the energy that comprises God.
19   We are quintessentially beings of energy.

Questions and/or Exercises:
- **Can you** see how we are all connected to the power?
- **Are you** aware that we use that power in creating everything in our lives—that we cannot do otherwise?
- **Can you** see how most of our creating is done by the unconscious part of our mind? Please don't give this one an unconscious monosyllable answer.
- **Doesn't the** fact that you are reading this book say you want that creation to be a conscious thing? *Tell me. Or better yet, tell yourself about it.*

The Truth of Our Being

The truth of our being requires no box, nor does it recognize its limits. The truth requires only the courage to face the unknown of possibility, the greatest of which is the possibility that we are, indeed, one with—and a physical part of—God!

"I am the creator." This is the one Law that those folks steeped in their religion will choke on. And it is not so much about accepting this Law. This Law *"just is,"* regardless of whether you accept it or not. What it takes to be courageous is found in the cost—the cost you will pay in the rejection by your friends and relatives, who don't accept it. Yes, this one takes *real courage!*

The lies you may live by demand validation from those who are close to you. But living the truth requires no such validation.

Keep breathing . . .

******

See Life's Laws:
1   I am the creator.
20   We are part of the energy that comprises God.

Questions and/or Exercises:
- **Do you** think that primitive people are steeped in superstition?
- **How many** of our current great religions began with primitive people?
- **Do you think** that just because we no longer consider ourselves as "primitive," and that our religions are generally termed as "organized," that we are no longer superstitious? ***Write about it.***

Putting the Shame on Sex

In general, our society—and especially our religions—demand that we hide the truth about sex from our children. By making it unacceptable in casual discussion, we hide it—even lie about its healthy nature. Is it any wonder the human race experiences sex with so much dysfunction?

In truth, sex is a gift from our Creator and a necessity for our very existence. Why does man curse it as wrong—the simple joy of it our religions term as evil, especially when not accompanied by promises and chains? Is it not simply the way God made us to be?

Why don't we treat it as a gift, one to another, and from God? Face it—the perceptions stem from our religions. By what pious insanity do religious leaders call God out as a liar? Does it not prove that they themselves, and their religions, are the real liars?

******

See Life's Laws:
15   One must do one's own thinking.
20   We are part of the energy that comprises God.
8   The world is not "out there"—it is "in here."

Questions and/or Exercises:
- **Did these** last two reflections blow you out of the water? Am I being too heavy-handed?
- **Is it** possible that when dealing with politics and religion, the truth often hurts?
- **Do you** know that this is why most Spiritual Law writers omit, or avoid dealing directly with these issues?
- **Would you** prefer I be like most? *Don't give yes or no answers. We're stepping into the real shit here—write about it.*

Good and Evil?

God, the great Omnipotent, everywhere within everything—

We hear our religions describing God so, and then turning around and limiting God to only the "good," and denying the part described as "evil." Then they would deny us our connection with God, saying God is a being somewhere "out there" in a place apart called "Heaven."

Could it be that they had it right in that first statement? And that we, too, are a part of God. And good and evil—the highest and lowest of the energy of it all—it is all there.

It is easy to see "evil" being a part of us. Yet we, in being a part of God in truth, have the choice of being evil or being love. This Earthly realm is where we choose to abide in God's love or not.

Here is where we make our choice to cut ourselves off from the flow of love—from God. To remain here in evil means this realm IS OUR HELL.

God—the Higher Power—does not make that choice in his/Her/Its realm; rather, WE make that choice HERE in this earthly realm called HELL.

Reincarnation? Yes. God's love gives us multiple chances to prove ourselves in evolving, in becoming love—in becoming as God in our own realm. In becoming one with experiencing infinity. Here in this earthly hell, we experience the sour so that we can evolve into the sweet of infinite love.

******

See Life's Laws:
20   We are part of the energy that comprises God.
3   Thoughts are energy: Loving, or not loving (fear).
4   The energy out, returns in kind.
8   The world is not "out there"—it is "in here."

Questions and/or Exercises:
- **Can you** appreciate the sweet, without knowing the sour?
- **Can God** appreciate the good, without knowing the evil?
- **Good—Evil?** Can we know either one, without it being within ourselves?
- **Can God?**—*All simple little questions, but deserving of a lot of ink.*

It Is All Good

One like-minded teacher says, *"It is all good."* I agree. It takes it all to make life: the good and bad—the right and wrong—the sweet and sour—and the love and the fear. We may be duality-minded, favoring only the more attractive end of each thing, but life requires it all. If we would but open our minds, we would see the truth in that simple saying:

"It is all good—it is all God."

And the alternative to life . . . is death. What then is it like? All "organized religions" claim to know what that looks like, and will freely tell you, despite their clear lack of experience. Just as they use your belief in a higher power to control you in life, so too do they threaten you with what will happen after death. Fear and control—that is all the preachers of organized religions have to offer.

Do my own New Thoughts beliefs in the truth of these laws offer more? While not the first to say these things, what I say in this book is offered with love, not fearful control. And I don't regard myself as a preacher. If you do, feel free to tell me to shut-the-fuck-up. I won't—but then I'm just a writer. And you don't have to be my reader. But as long as you choose to read, I don't have—or want—control over you.

Unlike Organized Religions, I have no interest in holding your spiritual balls hostage, nor in squeezing the life out of them.

✶✶✶✶✶✶

See Life's Laws
10   The purpose of life is for those lessons.
5   For every sorrowful thing, there exists the potential for equal joy. The Universe always balances.
16   We only control ourselves.
1   I am the creator.

Questions and/or Exercises:
- **In that** duality of our thinking, is it possible to appreciate anything in life without knowing its opposite? Can you see the perfection?
- **Do you** see how organized religions have always held us hostage to our belief in a higher power?
- **Is it still** so with you?
- **Of those** who have made their mark on history, how many did so, in defiance of the controlling religion?
- **For your** duality of mind, which is the more attractive: ***The Laws of Truth or Organized Religion?*** *They are, for the most part, opposites, y'know?*

Free Thinkers

There have always been thinkers—people who observe what happens in the world, correlate action to reaction, to results. And they listen to what other thinkers say and form their own conclusions. Just so, they listen to their heart and create their own personal connection to God.

Then there are those who just listen to what others say and accept it as fact. They are not thinkers. Some are just fools—following what their government leaders say is best for them. Some are just religious. For it would seem that what those who form religions do is demand all fools to believe as *they say* they themselves believe.

And God . . . Does God fit in there anywhere? Yes. God provides the "authority" that religions depend on, the sword that separates those foolish enough not to do their own thinking, from their personal freedom. The truth is, it is everyone's inalienable right to create their own beliefs, whether it be their connection with God or how they envision their world.

The questions to ask are these: Does that government leader do what is best for you? And do those religious leaders really believe what they say? Did God actually appear to one of them and tell them things? Or did someone just see an imaginary sword, to match an imaginary vision of a world, where they themselves wield the power of an all-powerful God—and use it? Then pass it all on, under whatever name they call their religion, a memorial to themselves.

The thinkers are seekers, and will always be free. Those who don't think, give up that freedom to those power mongers who thrive in religions and governments, and who are simply parasites.

And God? Isn't God all-powerful—beyond "want?" God created us all and gives us each the power and freedom to be who we choose to be—free thinker, foolish slave, or parasite. *So choose . . .*

✶✶✶✶✶✶

See Life's Laws:
8   The world is not "out there"—it is "in here."
1   I am the creator.
2   Thoughts Create.
13 Our own life is our sole possession. Just so, it is for everyone.
15 One must do one's own thinking.
16 We only control ourselves.

Questions and/or Exercises:
- **Do you** find these thoughts hard to swallow? Why?
- **Some would** say it is difficult to talk honestly about religion without appearing to bitch-slap it. Is this how you see it?
- **If so,** would it please you to move on to general spirituality? *Write down how you feel.*

Shepherds and Sheep

This thing called "Religion"—

It is what enables one man to influence others by the purity and the love that light his heart. It also allows another man to influence in the same way, but from the darkness and depravity of a malicious mind.

It will always be so, as long as we are but sheep, willing to be led by the crook of whichever shepherd holds the staff.

Whichever way it is—again—*religion* is but the *civilized* way of saying *superstition*. Both are used by those who would set themselves above it all, in order to control a primitive mind. The question then must be raised: Is your mind primitive? Or do you think for yourself?

Let's face it, folks; religion is really not so much about God, but rather it is about shepherds—and sheeples.

※※※※※※

See Life's Laws:
20   We are part of the energy that comprises God.
15   One must do one's own thinking.
13   Our own life is our sole possession. Just so, it is for everyone.

Questions and/or Exercises:
- **I know** for some, these things I say are often hard to swallow. You do know that no such demands are being made on you—not by me?
- **All I ask** is that you pay attention to **Law #15 above**—*so will you?*

The Ego's Expectations

Your ego's expectations of how it must be for you to get what you want will only guarantee you pain. What your ego wants and what your heart wants are very seldom the same. For your ego has eyes that can only look outward. It cannot see your heart within.

See Life's Law:
12—Our lives are run first by our needs, then our wants.

Questions and/or Exercises:
> ➤ **Do you** think your ego can ever be happy with what you have? *Can you? You are not your ego—there is a difference, y'know?*

>>><<<

Resurrections

As for the resurrection—for me, it has already come. I believe that the resurrection is indeed about an awakening to a new life, though not of the body. This awakening is of the mind—a change in consciousness. As such, it requires a death of sorts.

It is a remembering of who we are, and a taking of responsibility. And too, it is the death of blame. It is an ending of looking *out there*, for something or someone on which to place a *wrongness*, in order to own the *rightness*. And it is a beginning of looking *in here,* to the recognition of our own answers. The answers were always here.

******

See Life's Laws:
8   The world is not "out there"—it is "in here".
7   Blame is the abdication of responsibility.
15   One must do one's own thinking.

Questions and/or Exercises:
- **Do you** believe the "Resurrection" mentioned in the Bible is as a physical thing that most Christian religions say it is?
- **Or do you** think it is a change in consciousness like most "Spiritual" sects seem to think—myself included?

Designated Creator

Who knows what Gods our designated creators be? Still, in this life, it is I who am the creator. Yes! My God created this Earth, and everything in it. Still, of my own life, I get to create it—my way. But my creation is only of my own life, not of someone else's.

See Life's Laws:
1   I am the creator.
13   Our own life is our sole possession. Just so, it is for everyone.
20   We are part of the energy that comprises God.

Questions and/or Exercises:
- **Do you** get that the great downfall of pretty much all religions is that they *demand* you believe as they do?
- **Yes, this** book is how I see the Spiritual Laws to be. And no! I have no expectation that you will see it the same way. My request is that you take from this book only what works for you.

>>><<<

Everything We Need

Again: The Universe/God will always provide us with everything we need for our growth. Problem is: we only accept what we think we deserve.

******

See Life's Laws:
1   I am the creator.
2   Thoughts Create.
8   The world is not "out there"—it is "in here."

Questions and/or Exercises:
➢ **What has** this book provided you that you needed for your own personal growth? *Yes—write. . . .*

Soul Experience

It is one thing to learn something and *believe* it to be true; it is another thing to *know* it to be true. It is just so with our souls. There is nothing our souls do not know. Yet our soul needs the experience of it—here in this life—to *learn*, and to grow, and to know.

See Life's Law:
10   The purpose of life is for those lessons.

Questions and/or Exercises:
- **Ah, the** great meaning of this life thing—can you believe it is this simple?
- **What, if** anything, do you think is missing?

>>><<<

In Our Hearts

It's true! It is not enough to know a thing, up here, in our heads. Our soul is here to experience it; to learn it, as in our hearts. God knows it all. We are the life part, through which God gets to experience life and all life's feelings, as in the emotions of the heart. Just as we are God's taste buds experiencing life, so too do we experience the emotions of life, the feelings, for God's heart.

It is our job to learn, and in the experience to *know,* for the growth of our soul. And it is that through us, God can *know* life's emotional experiences as well. The events and people in our lives are merely there to give us lessons. The more emotional the feelings, the greater the gift for our soul. And perhaps the greater the experience, for the heart of God.

Yet for us here in this life, none of that matters if we are unwilling to accept the lessons of the gift offered and share them. Yes, when we don't accept the lessons, when we would rather blame others for our feelings rather than receive the gift, clearly, we cheat ourselves. Question is, do we also cheat God?

NO! A gift is a gift. And gifts have no strings, no expectations. It is always your choice to win or lose in your life. God does not lose—God does not win—God just experiences!

******

See Life's Laws:
18   Soul-to-soul pacts are made in the pre-existence.
10   The purpose of life is for those lessons.
20   We are part of the energy that comprises God.
7   Blame is the abdication of responsibility.

Questions and/or Exercises:
- **What is** God experiencing through you?
- **List the** top 10 or so things that come to mind that God experiences through you?
- *Now own them!*

Enlightenment and the Spiritual Warrior

Enlightenment is what happens when one shines the light of honesty upon oneself. It is to see clearly that we alone are the creators of our own life, and can no longer blame others for what we create, or how we feel about it.

Nor can we credit some supernatural force or being "out there" for all we might term good or evil about ourselves. Rather, enlightenment is to accept that it is we—ourselves—who are a mixture, incorporating at times either the energy of good, or evil, *loving, or unloving.* To be enlightened is to understand and accept that it is simply an internal choice in every moment of life.

Therefore, to be enlightened demands we fight an inner battle—become a Spiritual Warrior—those of us who would choose to be loving. For loving is the higher—yet is harder to maintain—of the two energies. Especially when facing the fears of others. However, loving has its own reward: *The Energy Out Returns in Kind*—remember?

******

See Life's Laws:
- 8   The world is not "out there"—it is "in here."
- 4   The energy out returns in kind.
- 7   Blame is the abdication of responsibility.
- 3   Thoughts are energy: Loving, or not loving (fear).
- 19   We are quintessentially beings of energy.
- 15   One must do one's own thinking.

Questions and/or Exercises:
- ➤ **Why exactly** did you get this workbook?
- ➤ **Were you** consciously wanting enlightenment?
- ➤ **If so,** did you know what the term meant?
- ➤ **If not,** do you know now? *Explain.*
- ➤ Do you have the courage required to be a Spiritual Warrior?

>>><<<

Shining Moments

Some of our most shining moments come when lighting up the darkness within us—that part we deem so odious, that even we don't want to see, much less smell it. Yet even the foulest of sewer gases can get ignited. It just takes a spark.

Or maybe for you, it is envisioned that within those dark regions of your mind there lies a powder keg, and that such a spark would blow all semblance of self-respect—indeed, your very life—to hell.

Yet, for those courageous enough to provoke such a spark, it does indeed provide light. Be it an exploding powder keg, sewer gas, or merely lighting the wick of a candle—doesn't matter. Within the light provided, we see and are inspired. There is no bliss more comforting than to bask in the knowledge of who we really are—to bask in the illumination of our soul.

And that "hell"—that unknown shame we believed was hidden within that fearful darkness? That shame was always our own personal hell, created by a fear-filled mind that did not know—or even consider—having courage.

✶✶✶✶✶✶

See Life's Laws:
8   The world is not "out there"—it is "in here."
19   We are quintessentially beings of energy.

Questions and/or Exercises:
- ➢ **Did this** help clear up that previous reflection *(Enlightenment and the Spiritual Warrior)? Explain.*
- ➢ **Are you** seeing who you are yet? Have you escaped your personal hell? *Tell yourself about it!*

>>><<<

Religion

Religion is the conscience of the thinking impaired.

It is the *right and wrong* for those who won't think for themselves—and are convinced that *right and wrong* somehow exist outside the judgmental minds of those "holier" than themselves.

See Life's Laws:
3   Thoughts are energy: Loving, or not loving (fear).
15   One must do one's own thinking.

Questions and/or Exercises:
- **Why do** I keep asking you to do your own fucking thinking?
- **Why is** it so important that I slap you upside the head with an F-bomb? *Write.*

>>><<<

Chicken Exits

You may recall how, in the Introduction, there was the following:

> *A note here for those who, like myself, are likely to get their sphincter all bound up over the linguistics of calling these things "Laws." Feel free to call them—"Principles" or "Truisms"—or any other word you choose.*

From what I am about to tell you, you may feel that I was setting you up to lose. NOT SO—I was setting you up to see something about you. Something that is true for everyone, but few want to recognize it for what it is: That "something" is our "chicken exits."

Have you ever been to a theme park where they feature that one *really scary ride?* Just before you get on that ride, you may have noticed a gate off to the side. That is the "chicken exit." It is for all those who thought they had the courage to do the ride, but at the last moment, *didn't.*

I wanted to give you your chicken exit—but one that would not keep you from taking this ride. Most people don't believe in absolutes. They think that there is always an exception to the rule. If at any point while reading *Book One or Two,* you felt that the law didn't apply, then the truth is, you made yourself the exception to the rule.

You took the chicken exit!

Again, these laws are like gravity: The only time gravity does not apply—the *apparent* exception—is when we are on an airplane that is in free-fall, or a spacecraft in orbit. "Apparent" because an orbit is simply a free-fall that keeps it falling around the Earth. If that spacecraft doesn't make occasional corrections, the orbit will deteriorate. And if the airplane does not restart its engines—well, the end result in both cases will be to crash and burn because gravity is still in effect. All laws have consequences for those who would break them. That is why they are called laws.

If you made yourself the exception to the laws and took any chicken exits, I want you to know that your life doesn't have to crash and burn. Start your engine back up and reapply these laws to your life as absolutes. Again, like gravity, they are absolutes. The crashing and burning—it is always your free choice to ignore the truth.

******

See Life's Laws:
All of them.

Questions and/or Exercises:
- **Did you** take any chicken exits?—If so, which ones?
- **Have** you gone back and applied the laws as absolutes? *Write about your thoughts on it.*
- **What in** particular did you have to acknowledge in order ***not*** to take that chicken exit?
- **Do you** regard this as "setting you up to lose"? Or is it a damned good lesson?

Your Conscious Choice

We are all full-spectrum souls. We have it *all* within us—everything from the meanest depths of depravity to the highest ecstasy of purest love. Were it not so, we could not recognize those things when exhibited by others.

How can a fish truly know the water until it gets out into the air? Now, given this knowledge, from this moment on, *you* are like that fish that has experienced the air. *You* now know something most others do not. In your journey through these pages, *you* now know the truth about life, about *yours*, and where *you* fit within the spectrum.

The good news is that *you* have the freedom to create *your* life. *You* get to choose just who *you* wish to be—indeed, who *you* are being. And if *you* aren't being everything *you* want—the "who" *you* want to be—*own it!* It is now your conscious choice. *Choose better.*

Yeah, looking at that one, for some, may be painful. If it's not exhilarating for *you*, then make it so. That, too, is now *your* conscious choice.

✶✶✶✶✶✶

See Life's Laws:
8   The world is not "out there"—it is "in here."
3   Thoughts are energy: Loving, or not loving (fear).
2   Thoughts Create.
25 Every word is an order to our soul.

Exercise:
- ➤ **Do you** wonder why I am leaning so hard on the word "you" in this reflection? Why do you think that is?
- ➤ *Write about the most important things you have learned from this book. You are summing up your growth here. Don't cheat yourself. Thoughts create, and every word—remember—is an order to your soul.*

About Beliefs

If you're not getting what you want, you need to remember that you are getting what you believe you can have. The Universe is built to perform according to your beliefs.

✶✶✶✶✶✶

See Life's Laws:
2   Thoughts Create.
4   The energy out returns in kind.

Questions and/or Exercises:
- **What don't** you have that you want?
- **What is** it about you that says you can't have it?
- **No**—**we** are talking about your beliefs—your thinking. ***Write about that.***

▶▶▶◀◀◀

You Are the Winner!

Among all those countless billions—no, trillions, maybe even quadrillions of souls in this infinite universe—you have won the lottery! You get to live a life on one of the greatest planets in existence—Earth. And more, this life is lived as a member of the most advanced species on the planet. *But hey, you do know that everything worth having comes with a price—remember?*

Now, the fact that you are reading, that you even can read, says that you have been enjoying your prize for a time now. Have you recognized the price yet? How so many of those other winners also enjoying their own lives, believe they are entitled, that you owe them a piece of your prize.

For instance, it is common for parents to expect you to live your life as they do, to demand you carry on yours exactly as they would—that you be the next "them."

And those folks you rub shoulders with every day, how most will expect you to live and think the same way they do—even though it causes them no harm if you don't?

Oh, and that one special one—that "significant one"—how he or she will likely demand that you allow them to control your life, to force you to live it to suit themselves, so that they will choose to feel good about who you are effortlessly.

Yes, pretty fucked-up, wouldn't you say? This whole entitlement thing has always been the norm, but these days it has been re-labeled, "progressive thinking"—even though it leaves no room for the progress of a person's soul.

And then there is your religion. It especially expects you to live this sacred prize—your life—the way they demand. Maybe that is because they would wield the power of the universe, the power of God—*if you would let them.* They would convince you that everything good you get is a gift from God—but only if you bow to their evangelical line of bullshit.

Of course, all the bad stuff? That comes from those other mundane souls around you, or from your government, or even just this world. If you step too far out of their clutches, they threaten you with some mystical beast they call "The Devil," who will torture you with fire—a bit superstitious, don't you think?

Of them all, they want you to be held captive to their wishes—a slave. They all demand that you give your life to them. They want you to believe you are a victim, same like them.

But you? You have won the lottery once more. You have discovered the truth. Among them all, you are one of the rare conscious ones. But with nearly everyone you know—even those close who have sworn their love to you—you will find the price for you to think differently is often found in their inability to then accept you.

You've read this book. And while it doesn't tell you much that you mightn't have read in other books, perhaps this one you read with your heart, and not just your mind. Possibly, in seeing the price you pay—probably are already paying—you can see the great value in these truths.

Painful? Yes, but pain is one of those indicators the Higher Power of the universe has given us to point out the way. Here on Earth, you don't *win;* rather, you *earn* that next great lottery. You are one of the few who have learned the lessons, seen the lies, and experienced the truth of life—and evolved your soul through that experience. You might not see it, or believe this yet, but you will. *And you will find that the price was worth it!*

******

See Life's Laws:
This reflection encompasses every one of the laws as given.

Questions and/or Exercises:
- **The price** is high—I paid it too. Most authors writing about Spiritual Laws omit telling you the whole truth. Are you glad I did? *Write about it.*
- **Much of** what this book tells you—including this—is repeated in different scenarios. Did this work for you? Or is this the first time you truly heard it—in your heart and not just your head? *Again, write about it.*

➢ **Y'know, a** lot of folks don't get the point until the scenario matches up with their lives. Did you get that match-up earlier? *Yup. Write, tell yourself about it.*

Now On to the Next Lottery

Are you feeling pretty special for having won these last two lotteries? Are you ready to win the next one—the one where you will evolve beyond it all?

You are here on Earth, and you have realized your connection to the power of all the Universe—that you are, in actuality, a part of God. And you have taken responsibility for your life and everything in it.

Undoubtedly, you have even begun to share your love in the service of those who need you. What more can there be to evolve into without dying? It is a simple thing, really—*it is to touch the love of that God-part within you.*

What?—What the fuck does that mean?

It is not something you learn, not something you do, not even something for you to "be." It is something you *feel* with all the passion of your being—GRATITUDE!

Gratitude for all you have become. Gratitude for all who have played their respective parts for you—or you for them—in life. Most of all, gratitude for the beauty of all that the Higher Power has immersed you in your life.

> *The wind through your hair.*
> *The never-to-be-repeated shapes in the clouds above.*
> *The raindrops on your face.*
> *And afterwards, the clean smell of ozone in the air.*
> *The buzz of a honey bee, adding to your life its own special sweetness.*
> *The flight of a hummingbird.*
> *The colors of its plumage, and of the flowers from which it sips.*
> *Or of the rainbow in the distant sky.*
> *Then there is the gold of a sunset—and the joy that comes with the next sunrise.*

Whatever price you have—or will—pay for changing your mind, consider it worth it: PAID, done deal. EVERYTHING in this world—and every experience you have, you now get to meet with GRATITUDE.

Your life means nothing without it!

See Life's Laws:
Again, this one needs no laws listed in explanation—and no questions asked—it just needs one exercise. You know what that one is—

>>><<<

The Choice

In all the Universe, in the whole infinite vastness of it all, what is there if there is not life? And Life? What is life, if there is not sentience—self-aware, feeling, thinking, creative intelligence?

Some believe the Universe—the all-encompassing whole of it all—is God, the omnipotent, all-powerful, within everything, everywhere, everywhen . . . *that God!* And everywhere in the Universe that life can develop, it does. Does it not appear that throughout it all, that God is geared toward bringing forth life? And life? Again, what is the pinnacle of life, if it is not sentience? Would that not describe us?

And if we are of such importance—or perhaps pleasure—for God, then wouldn't God want to nurture us? Wouldn't God give us the ability to hope and dream and conceive? And, wouldn't that say that God serves us? So why do religions say that we are only here to serve God? Does God, the omnipotent, all-powerful everything, really need someone, who those religions would place outside of God's all-encompassing self, to be a servant? Or do we merely serve as one, inside, together?

Consider: We are all part of the energy of the Universe—part of God—aren't we? Assuming that the energy of the Universe IS God—and being a part of God called sentient life, how do we fit into it all? Could it be that we are the taste buds by which God gets to feel/taste/experience life? For what is sentient life, if not thinking, feeling, experiencing beings? And can one know the sweet, without tasting the sour? Can one ever feel the loving if there is not some opposite, fearful *other* thing?

And doesn't cultivating this buffet require that we have free choice in our feelings and in our being?

Yes WE, being a part of this all-encompassing wholeness, that many, including I, believe is "God,"—WE, being the highest, sentient pinnacle of the life part of creation—WE get to choose to be the best, or the worst of God's life experiences—WE get to be the sweet or the sour.

So . . . make your choice! *Do you want to be the loving or the non-loving experience of God? And remember—where, and to what, and to whom the loving part leads you into being.*

✱✱✱✱✱✱

See Life's Laws:
3   Thoughts are energy: Loving, or not loving (fear).
5   For every sorrowful thing, there exists the potential for equal joy. The Universe always balances.
20   We are part of the energy that comprises God.
24   What we dwell upon with energy is what we attract.
4   The energy out returns in kind.

Questions and/or Exercises:
- **How much** of your life do you spend in the energy of love, as opposed to fear?
- **Knowing that** you are as a taste-bud by which God tastes life, will that ratio now be changing?
- *List everything about yourself that is sweet.*

Taste Buds of God

What does it all mean? Here at the end, let me leave you with a few personal thoughts—some crudely esoteric redneck shit—shit that you may think stinks.

In Book One, there is a reflection entitled "Fear." It was explained that there is a duality that we insist on defining everything as being between. And in the center, there is a tipping point—as in between sweet and sour, there is tasteless. Between love and fear, there is indifference. Is it possible that God resides at that tipping point—or maybe in the center of an infinitely large circle of life? Clearly at a place that is beyond our understanding—mine, yours, everyone's. . . .

Is God simply an infinite indifference—a point of tastelessness—a neediness? Is that why God is so bent on creating life: Life that can and does fill that space with our choice of energy—love or fear? Are we indeed the taste buds of God, experiencing life? Or more—maybe we are God's entertainment system?

God is the great enigma. Who, how, or what is God? It's all speculation—us, trying to make sense of the indefinable—something beyond our ability to understand.

Here's a real redneck speculation: What if God were like a big cat licking its fur? Would Mankind be as a fur-ball in that cat's shit—shit that has nourished the cat. Now that statement will make a few folks cough in indignation. Still, what if. . . .

Point being: If anyone tells you they KNOW what God is, just picture a big turd of hairy cat shit they've painted pink—because that is what that person has between their ears. NO one knows what God is.

Irreverent? Me—irreverent? Indeed, not where God is concerned. Although I believe God would be way beyond any need for our reverent worshipful adulation. To me, God just is. Does He/She/It care about what we think? Personally, I think God only cares that we feel and experience life. Where we are concerned, maybe God has a cat-shit sense of humor.

Acccchhhh—errraacccchhhh—aaaaachhhhttt.

Excuse me while I hack up this hairball. Wouldn't want it to become immersed in all that shit between my own ears. That's right! Haven't I, too, been telling you who God is?

I, too, simply don't know. I believe you've got to die to truly know. What I do know is that I have been to the edge of that cliff and have caught a glimpse—but only a small one. One just large enough to help me see through all this "religion" crap and to know a little of the truth.

The truth?—It can be anal-ogized to WD 40. That's right—the penetrating oil. It can seep down through even the smallest crack. Like truth, if the vessel has any holes in it, WD 40 will leak through. These rules—these Laws—are the vessels I've found that will hold truth.

Is God—as many believe—composed of all the energy of the universe? Or is God something else, maybe the space between and all around all those particles of that energy, an eternal nothingness that is everything?

The enigma . . .the unfathomable . . . the indefinable . . . the. . . .
Hell, does it really matter? For us mortals, what matters is the truth. The lies we have all been taught to believe, just . . . DON'T . . . FUCKING . . . WORK. The truth does.

I told you in the beginning that I wouldn't lie—nor tell you half-truths. I bet you didn't expect all this here at the end. Sounds almost like a disclaimer.

So now, let me take this on out there into the outfield, with some of my own personal beliefs. Thing is, these Spiritual Laws? They've been around probably since the dawn of religion and before—ever since our kind began to understand that there must be some higher power, some intelligence much greater than us.

These Spiritual Laws of Truth operate on the principle that we are a part of—in fact, a piece of that higher power. And that we actually wield that power in the very creation of our own lives. You may have seen the movie or read the book, *The Secret*. If you did, you probably recognized it in the laws presented here in this book, only expressed differently.

Spiritual Law #1—
I am the creator.

It is exactly—and literally so. We do create our lives, and we do it with our thoughts.

And religions?—So long as we can make the connection with that Higher Power in our minds, does it really matter? It is not for me to say that your religion is false, that it is wrong. But what I think is dysfunctional is the greed and lust for power in some of the men— or women—who would use your beliefs in that religion for personal gain or glory.

Yes, given that we actually wield the power of creation, although in this mortal life, we wield it slowly. What about when we leave this mortal body and are a spirit, *a Soul on that God level?* Wouldn't it be logical that we would then wield it instantly?

And of God, *the Great Essence of the Infinite*—can you see that while we know in our heads about infinity, we do NOT know it in our hearts? Has anyone alive ever experienced it? Infinity is beyond the grasp—the understanding—of us mere mortals. So why can't all religions be true, at least in their beliefs concerning the afterlife? Isn't it safe to say that pretty much all religions are concerned with, and have at least some beliefs about an afterlife?

In that afterlife, why can't Catholics have their Catholic heaven— even their hell? Mormons don't believe in hell, but why would that stop them from having their three degrees of glory—all of it exactly as they believe? And can it not also be so for all other religions with their beliefs?

Even Islam—as I understand it, the Koran doesn't specify, but some Muslim men are being promised seventy-two virgin wives. Not to insult their Heaven—all I can say is that they must be more man than I. That many wives would wear me down to a stub in no time. Gotta wonder what I'd do with the rest of eternity

Me? I know that eventually I will be punching out on the great time clock of life. And I believe in reincarnation—so as Arnold says, ". .

. I'll be back." But unlike many others who also hold this belief, it won't be as a bug.

And God?—Perhaps my God is only limited to the ability of my personal perceptions. This book is only meant to open your mind to the infinite possibilities—not to limit it by my own. My own personal truth about God is my own—yours is yours. *It doesn't . . . fucking . . . matter . . . if they don't match.*

So long as it doesn't, then that makes us—you and me—organized religion's greatest nightmare. Religions are in the business of separating us from God and then selling God back a little piece at a time.

And religions require that everyone have ONLY one truth concerning a Creator. They still—to this day—are killing one another over something so esoterically fucked-up.

Governments want control of your life—religions want control of your mind. Both want to steal your money.

I vote for who I want in government—ignore organized religion—and the money? Hell, we all pay a fair share to run the hog farm.

For the most part, my life is peaceful and happy. I run it mostly on love, and—to the best of my ability—observe the Spiritual Laws.

If you can grasp that, perhaps God has taught you something about experiencing infinity—or maybe just in making your own choices on how you choose to think and feel. But hey . . . it's just a thought. And we know what Spiritual Law says about thoughts now, don't we?

******

See Life's Laws:
This is pure personal speculation—based on all the Laws as this redneck understands them. Why else title this book **Redneck Spirituality?**

Questions/exercises to consider:
- ➤ **Write down** *your own thoughts and speculations. Unless you want to write your own book, limit it to 10—or maybe 15,000 words.*

➤ **If you've** used this space to take offense—this far in—ya gotta know that I've failed you as a companion on your journey. ***Write about that.***

If you did, there is a concept in this book titled "taking offence." Re-read it. Did you agree, or did you double down? Write about that.

One and The Same

When you want to hurt someone—when you want revenge—ask yourself, is this what I would want to do, if he were me? For he is you, y'know?

And I am too. You're hurting all of us. Like love, hurt is a feeling we give to ourselves. It too has nothing to do with others. Yet it too is felt by all. On that level beyond consciousness, we are all one and the same—you and I—and all of humanity.

And too—Aren't we also a part of God? Must take pretty big balls to put the hurt on God?

******

See Life's Laws:
20   We are part of the energy that comprises God.
1   I am the creator.
4   The energy out returns in kind.
19   We are quintessentially beings of energy.

Questions and/or Exercises:
- **What do** you believe God—that Higher Power—is?
- **There is** order—structure—and laws that govern the workings of the Universe. God perhaps? *What do you think?*
- **Are we** not all part of the energy of the Universe? *Any thoughts on that?*

Epilogue

Both books in this series are an in-your-face redneck experience. I wrote them that way on purpose. Most folks will never get honest about their lives until the shit's in their face. Even then, they don't like to acknowledge the truth of it. That truth is just as this title suggests. Shit points out what stinks in life. So, take it on home—*in your life.*

You've got that correctly—this book is about your life, about looking at it and learning those lessons—the ones right now in your face. And yes! They're gonna stink.

Again, shit is what's nourished you. Doesn't matter if that shit is coming out of your butt, or leaking from between your ears. Difference is, when coming from one end, it just needs to be flushed. But when from the other—yeah, it's gonna stink, and it is gonna be in your face. To flush it, you're gonna need to change something in your thinking. And that is gonna change your whole life. And too, what your life then becomes, doesn't stink.

Skid stains across your face or in your shorts—do you really want to meet the Angel of Death with either end stinking? Going to your grave is a sure thing. The stinking is not.

What Then

When I die . . .when I'm dead . . .what then?
Who will be there to watch the ashes fall?
Into space . . . into eternity.
To mix and become one with the good red soil,
in the cool shady canyons
beneath those magnificent,
sheer sandstone cliffs . . .
the ancient homeland,
of the Anasazi.

Perhaps I was one, in a former life.
I feel a kinship there, a homecoming.
And what of this life?
Will there be a hole
in the fabric of humanity?
Whose lives have I touched?
Is this world a better place
because I drew breath?
Will there be multitudes
to shed bitter tears?

Or will it be a mere blink,
a single tick of the clock of humanity,
before all remembrance
and trace of me will vanish?
Except for a fragment of bone,
lodged under a rock
in some dry watercourse . . .

Or a few molecules of magnesium
nurturing a cedar . . .
Potassium in a flower . . .
Or perhaps, some calcium in the
tooth of a playful little chipmunk.
I will become a part of, and one,
with the canyon lands.
It is enough. . . .

And sometime perhaps,
my soul will reincarnate.
And I will once again
walk these desert plateaus . . .
drink from the cool springs,
deep in the shadowy canyons.
And perhaps,
I will sit in the shade of a cedar. . .
Admire the perfection of a wild flower. . .
Even laugh at the antics
of a joyful little chipmunk.
And perhaps, I already have—

The question for you is not "WHAT THEN," it is WHAT NOW? You wouldn't be reading this book if you were not becoming aware of the lies we have all been taught upon which we "should" base our lives. You are searching for truth—and you have found some.

You are now forever changed.
You now know truths
you cannot deny.

Oh you may slip and slide around a little, but you will always come back to these truths. And you will find yourselves living them. Your life will become much more peaceful and functional— although many of the people who were once there will be gone. And some will be missed.

Those who replace them will also be loved.
For you now know better how to love.
And when "what then" eventually comes,
you will rejoice in the life you have lived

FROM NOW.

About The Assessment

At this point, you might consider whether you have read and done the exercises in **Book One.** If you have not, I highly recommend that you do so **now**. If you will do that, then do **NOT** turn this page and finish this assessment now. For if you do,

YOU WILL BE CHEATING YOURSELF.

The Assessment

Go back through your workbook/s and reassess those reflections upon which you placed a circle of resistance. If you find you no longer feel that resistance, then checkmark it—and it is okay if you still have resistance.

For those who have chosen not to do Book One, the following is necessary information from that book: These workbooks are not about being *right* or *wrong*. I hope you can see and understand that by this point. This book is *only* about seeing the workings of the Spiritual Laws—*The Laws of Truth* in your life. It does not have to be the same for *you* as it is for me. The point of this book is to give you some real truth —*the Laws*— and then to get you to look within yourselves.

This assessment is to tell you if it did that, and if there has been any change in your thinking. If there has, then this book has been instrumental in changing your life—*change your mind, change your life*. Remember?

In the beginning, you were asked to get a notebook, preferably one that is a binder, to do the questions and exercises. You were asked to write only on the right-hand pages. Here is one further exercise for you. Consider doing this one with a different colored ink pen.

Exercise:

> ➢ Go over the original questions and answers. If there are any you would now answer differently, put a line through those parts you would change, and use the blank left side sheets to write in your changes. Having since gone through this book and hashed out the meanings of how the laws apply, any changes you make here are an indication of how you have evolved—and know, this doesn't mean your original answer was wrong. There is no right or wrong, remember. There is only truth and love—or not love. What this assessment indicates is how much better you now see truth, and how much more capacity you now have to love.

Now for the most important part of this exercise

At the beginning of this assessment, you were asked to check off those circles of resistance. Take special note of any reflections you might have marked with an exclamation point. Have you checked them off, or do you still feel resentment? If you do, then that's okay. Just understand: There is no attack intended with anything I have written here. And even if you think you see an attack, you have to admit that it cannot possibly be an actual physical thing.

Correct?

A physical attack must be met with resistance. Any other attack is only one of perception—*your own perception*—regardless of what you think was the other person's intent. Perceiving it as an attack is how people who see themselves as victims ensure they will be. If you are still taking offense, then the working part of both books *now must ask its most important question:*

Questions—Just one to consider:
➢ *How much longer do you intend to see yourself as a victim in life?*

You see, the basic premise of these spiritual laws is the truth—that being, it is a choice. We have all been taught to be victims in life.

**AND THE TRUTH IS: WE ARE NOT!
WE ARE THE CREATORS.**

Do you not yet understand what that means? It means that we are WHO we want to be, and we HAVE what we want to have in life. If it is not what we think we want, then we must seek out the truth of why it serves us.

BECAUSE IT DOES SERVE US!

You will almost always see that if it goes against Spiritual Law, it is because we are choosing to see ourselves as that victim we were taught to be.

**IT IS A CHOICE:
To be the VICTIM, or the CREATOR.**

The service being a victim gets you, is that you don't have to be responsible for anything, and you get to suck up the sympathy of others, like a **PSYCHIC VAMPIRE**.

Let's look at the truth:

- Only **VICTIMS** resent!
- Only **VICTIMS** take offense.
- Only **VICTIMS** go crying to others—sucking up their energy for validation.

When you get fully disgusted with being a psychic vampire—blaming others, and believing yourself a victim—

YOU WILL CHANGE.
And you will then become a true

CREATOR.

>>><<<

About The Author

Publishers prefer this section to be written in the third person, even though it is generally written by the author. No lies, remember?

These days, how much of what politicians say can you take as "truth?" It is the same with those in academia. Most are just "talking heads" when it comes to what's true in life. Unless or until they have learned the truth in their real life, they don't . . . fucking . . . "know."

Speaking of real life, folks like me don't . . . fucking . . . look—not until they are faced with the reality of their own death. You won't find any letters of accolade behind my name, except for the one on this book's title page—and that one, only because it is the name by which some have known me.

About now, you might be saying to yourself, "Oh my God, what's this about the 'F' bomb?" Yes, I'm a redneck, and sometimes we use that bomb to wake people up.

The story of my life can be found in Book One. But Book Two is more advanced—that being said, here is the "rest of the story."

Twenty-five years ago, while lying in a hospital bed, knowing the imminent presence of death, I realized my life had been no more than skid marks in the shorts of the life I *wished* I'd lived. I swore an oath to that "presence" that whatever life might remain would be used in searching out life's great truths, and becoming someone such as would fill those shorts without stain or stink—a tall order for someone who had no clue how.

I was only just beginning to see my life's lies. So I started hanging out with others also searching for truth: New Age, New Thought groups, meditating, and reading books about truth—about Spiritual Law.

Then, for several years, I worked on the support teams for one of the two personal growth—experiential—seminars companies with which I had experience. By then, my life was based on these Spiritual Laws, and had become peaceful and functional.

Wanting to pass that on to others, I took accredited coach training from Coach University, and upon graduating, opened a practice as a Personal Life Coach.

Coaching clients in finding the joy missing from their lives was immensely satisfying during those years—the head-hunting part required to make it lucrative was not. Then, for the next twelve years, I drove Para Transit buses, taking people with various disabilities where they needed to go. Most desperately needed the help, and for me, being of service to them was also gratifying.

I seldom coach one-on-one these days. Mostly now, it is with these written words. Still, Coaches need a clear contract, an admission by the client that they want the coaching, and preferably are willing to pay for it. I take it on faith that I have that contract with you—hopefully you bought this book—and after all, you are still spending time reading it.

None of this negates the fact that I am a redneck. And rednecks generally love motorcycles—a fifty-year love affair for me. This fact weighs heavily on the reason for this writing.

Riding alone is enjoyable, and riding with others who share like-minded joys is even more so. As one of the original five who started up the American Legion Riders in Nevada. Through my connections in the ALR, I later became the first Nevada State Captain for the Patriot Guard.

Started for the purpose of non-violently protecting funerals from religious zealots, and to honor our nation's heroes who have paid that ultimate price of freedom, the Guard was a fine, even cathartic, experience for me.

But for me, it was—at least in part—a pressing need. My own service during the Vietnam "conflict" was as a sole survivor. Since just after WW II—1948—the armed services have had a policy that when notified that a soldier is the last surviving male member in a family, the parents can apply for that status, and their son will not be stationed in a war zone. I did not know until years later that mine had.

There are 58,267 casualties listed on the Vietnam Memorial Wall—and that does not count the suicides, Agent Orange, and war wound deaths that occurred later. Reflecting on how I floated past Vietnam on a free pass always came with a sense of shame.

Honoring those making the ultimate sacrifice in this current war, for me, became a very personal thing. It was akin to honoring that GI back then, who might have died in my place.

Most of the thoughts in this book were written years ago and considered private. There was little inclination felt to share them—until my experiences in the Patriot Guard. It shook me to the core to stand in flag lines with a hundred other teary-eyed patriots, mostly rough, tattooed veteran bikers, like myself, to honor yet another fallen hero. And then to realize: It is the consciousness of this world that makes such a sacrifice necessary.

> *And I knew about consciousness—knowledge I'd written so much about, but wasn't sharing in any appreciable way.*

The Patriot Guard was a healing experience in my life, but nothing comes without a price. After meeting the presence of the Angel of Death, I learned those laws of truth and began living my life accordingly. But life balances—being no longer acceptable by my loved ones was the price I paid for seeing life differently.

Those who are closest to you are usually there because your thinking validates their own. I was no longer pretending to be that "good Mormon son"—or the limp-dick controllable husband.

All I've ever had on this earth is my life, and not enough time to live it. But living it my way—with love and joy—was not acceptable to those who wanted my life lived their way. Even so, that price was paid long before the Patriot Guard. And that price was worth it.

In the Patriot Guard Riders—besides tears—the price of my healing included physical pain and discomfort. There were icy winter winds numbing my cheeks, freezing my fingers, and chilling my shaking body as I rode north in twenty-three-degree weather to honor another hero killed in action. My misery seemed equal to that of the silent yucca trees parading past, their tortured arms up in frozen salute.

And later, with a blistering summer sun doing its best to liquefy the tar in the pavement beneath my wheels, I carried my nation's flag for many more final salutes—other heroes KIA. Here too was pain as the twin pipes of my exhaust baked this veteran's chestnuts, and the rush of scorching air coming off that highway stung my finger tips, while the burning steel of the grips blistered the palms of my hands.

And then there was the sweat that trickled down my butt crack, moistening—but not staining—my shorts.

But none of this was more uncomfortable than the shame of not doing all I knew I could.

For me, there is joy in holding my life in the twist of my grip on the throttle. Knowing I am the absolute creator, in riding my own life's highway, and feeling the thundering rumbling power with the clench of my butt cheeks in the saddle. But now I can no longer shirk my responsibility. It is now time to just fart and get on with it, and to share this—my own simple attempt to raise the consciousness of anyone riding behind. Perhaps you might be inclined to view that fart, imparted between the pages of this book in all its glorious crudity, as the sad bottom line of my life.

Not me—this is not the skidmarks of my bottom line, rather this ink represents the highest and best I've ever been.

And crudity? If this redneck is anything like the rest, crudity is simply a coping mechanism for dealing with those heart-wrenching moments. Perhaps you can decide on the truth of that matter for yourself—and forgive me for the crudity of my humanity.

Or maybe, forgive yourselves—those of you inclined to make my humanity somehow . . . wrong?

Despite all that inspired me in writing this book, it is not about me, or my redneck crudity—not even about skid-marks. It is about you. YOU: another soul who wants to love, and be loved—*without the pink paint.* It is about you too, being the best you can be, showing up in the naked honesty of who you are right here—

RIGHT NOW.

NOTES

NOTES

NOTES

NOTES

NOTES

NOTES

NOTES

www.ingramcontent.com/pod-product-compliance
Lightning Source LLC
Chambersburg PA
CBHW020055020526
44112CB00031B/175